Understanding Spelling

'[This book] should be part of every school's library and a course book for every postgraduate course … It is a splendid, sound and helpful book which has a thoughtful but practical approach.'

Dr Eve Bearne, *University of Cambridge Faculty of Education*

'An essential buy for many trainee teachers. For schools, [this book] would assist the literacy coordinator in advising staff to help others teach spelling more effectively.'

Professor Teresa Cremin, *Canterbury Christ Church University College*

How do children learn to spell and what kinds of teaching support them most effectively?

Based on a three-year longitudinal study of children's spelling in different primary classrooms, this book poses a number of questions.

- What kinds of knowledge are involved in spelling?
- What are the links between learning to read and learning to spell?
- What kinds of systematic teaching and interventions make a difference to children's progress?

Packed with case studies, photographs and examples of children's work, this unique book sets out the most effective approaches to spelling and provides teachers with a broad set of principles on which to base their teaching. This is an invaluable resource for any teacher or trainee teacher wishing to raise standards in spelling in their classroom.

Olivia O'Sullivan is currently Assistant Director of the Centre for Literacy in Primary Education.

Anne Thomas is the former Inset Director of the Centre for Literacy in Primary Education.

Understanding Spelling

Olivia O'Sullivan
Anne Thomas

Routledge
Taylor & Francis Group
LONDON AND NEW YORK

Centre for Literacy in Primary Education

First published 2007
by Routledge
2 Park Square, Milton Park, Abingdon, Oxon, OX14 4RN

Simultaneously published in the USA and Canada
by Routledge,
270 Madison Ave, New York, NY 10016

An earlier version of this book was originally published by the CLPE in 2000.

Routledge is an imprint of the Taylor & Francis Group, an informa business

© 2000, 2007 CLPE

Photographs by Phil Polglaze

Typeset in Garamond by Bookcraft Ltd, Stroud, Glos

Printed and bound in Great Britain by Bell & Bain Ltd, Glasgow

British Library Cataloguing in Publication Data
A catalogue record for this book is available from the British Library

Library of Congress Cataloging in Publication Data
Understanding spelling / Olivia O'Sullivan and Anne Thomas.
    p. cm.
    Includes bibliographical references.
    1. Spelling ability—England—London—Longitudinal studies. 2. English
    language—Orthography and spelling—Study and teaching (Elementary)—
    England—London—Longitudinal studies. I. Thomas, Anne, 1932- II. Title.
LB 1574.078 2007
372.63'2—dc22   2006036311

ISBN10: 0-415-41988-3 (pbk)
ISBN10: 0-203-96161-7 (ebk)
ISBN13: 978-0-415-41988-8 (pbk)
ISBN13: 978-0-203-96161-7 (ebk)

Contents

Foreword

This edition of *Understanding Spelling* will be published seven years after the first edition, which was itself based on a three-year research project. It is interesting therefore to reflect on what has happened to the teaching and learning of spelling since then.

The National Literacy Strategy (NLS) (DfES, 1998), introduced in the final year of our research, and now in the process of revision, contained many of the teaching approaches highlighted in our project for the effective teaching of spelling. The NLS also highlighted wider aspects of English spelling which, as our research showed, become increasingly important in Key Stage 2, such as the role of meaning and grammar within English spelling, through compound words, prefixes, suffixes, word roots and origins.

What we have found, however, in courses and inservice training sessions is that many teachers are still unsure about how children learn to spell. Many find difficulty addressing the needs of all children in their classes and lack confidence in how to intervene in children's spelling, particularly when there are difficulties in making progress. There has also been a continuing lack of appreciation for the different routes children might take into the spelling system in the early stages, as exemplified in the case studies presented in Chapter 5.

Several issues arose which became causes for concern. First there was a lack of time for children to write. This was partly due, in the earlier stages of the NLS, to restrictions imposed by the timings of the literacy hour but was also due to other curriculum pressures. The restriction on time was particularly important given the relationship which our research project uncovered between frequent opportunities to write at some length and the positive effects on children's spelling progress. After two or three years of the strategy, some schools began to introduce longer writing sessions where children could write more extensively, but lack of time for writing and the achievement gap between reading and writing, particularly in the case of boys, became a cause for national concern. Several research and development projects have addressed this broader issue, which is wider than our core concern of spelling, but which has important effects on children's spelling, if they can be encouraged and inspired to write (Barrs and Pidgeon, 2000; Safford, O'Sullivan and Barrs, 2004; UKLA/PNS, 2004).

Second, greater emphasis on the teaching of 'word level' work, i.e. spelling and phonics, put a greater emphasis on spelling, but there has been a continuing tendency at all levels to muddle the processes involved in learning to spell and learning to read, a complex relationship explored at some length in this book (Chapters 3 and 4). In the last few years there has been a growing emphasis on the role of phonics in learning to read which has sometimes led to an overemphasis on 'sounding out' as an approach to spelling. This has been at the expense of adopting a broader range of strategies from early on, including looking at words, or helping young children to think about the structure of words. During inset sessions and courses we have found that one of the most effective ways of persuading adults to appreciate the different kinds of knowledge and strategies involved in spelling unfamiliar words is to carry out a spelling test. Adults who are put in the position of children by having to spell unfamiliar words quickly realise that there is much more to spelling than 'sounding out'. The Qualifications and Curriculum Authority (QCA), which comments on children's progress in end of Key Stage SATs, has also continued to point out the importance of a wider range of spelling strategies. For example in 2002, reviewing children's progress in spelling in SATs at the end of Key Stage 2 it urged teachers to teach children to

- use their knowledge of word roots to ensure the correct spelling vowels, e.g. vanish/vaneshing; injure/injered;
- learn ways to check their accuracy when adding prefixes and pronunciation of swimming/swiming, regardless/regardles.

(QCA, 2002)

And in 2005, QCA asked teachers in Key Stage 1 to teach children to:

- use correct plural forms of nouns, e.g. boxes, branches
- learn when to double the consonant when adding a suffix, e.g. running.

(QCA, 2005)

Finally, there is still uncertainty about what is involved in teaching spelling. Our research found that successful teachers took a view of spelling which went far beyond teaching a group of words or a spelling pattern and testing it. They created a climate of interest and involvement in words for all children, and set up a range of classroom contexts and routines for working on spelling. Although, to its credit, the NLS emphasised an active approach to teaching spelling and offered helpful teaching materials, the structure of the *NLS Framework for Teaching* (DfES, 1998), with its welter of teaching objectives, tended to obscure some of the key teaching routines which help children to acquire independence as spellers. Chapter 6 of *Understanding Spelling* sets out teaching approaches for Key Stage 1 and Reception (children aged 5–7) and Key Stage 2 (children aged 7–11), under such headings as 'Classroom contexts', 'Resources', 'Main classroom routines for teaching spelling', 'Class and group activities to develop spelling knowledge', 'Routines to establish independence', in a way that has proved to be of enormous value to teachers and teaching assistants. Our project also highlighted social and collaborative aspects of learning to spell which prove highly effective for children, such as working with an editing partner, or working with a partner to learn spellings.

For all these reasons we are happy that *Understanding Spelling*, originally published by the Centre for Literacy in Primary Education, is being re-published by Routledge. We are hopeful that our research – including the findings, theoretical discussions, case studies and practical approaches for teaching and monitoring children's progress as spellers – continues to have much to offer to all those working in schools.

Olivia O'Sullivan and Anne Thomas
March 2007

Acknowledgements

We are very grateful to the Mercers' Company in the City of London for their sponsorship of this project and for their support and interest throughout.

We offer our deepest thanks to the headteachers and staff of the project schools for their commitment, collaboration and support over the three years of the project, during which time they managed to make time for us despite many pressures on them.

We are indebted to the case study children for their willingness to share their writing and ideas and for all we have learned from them.

We thank Myra Barrs, former Director of CLPE, for her work with us on editing this book and thank all the staff at CLPE for their support for and interest in the project.

We thank Ann Lazim for her work on the bibliography.

We thank Phil Polglaze for his photography; all images are his copyright.

Chapter 1

Introduction

This book is the result of a three-year longitudinal study of children's spelling. The project was sponsored by the Mercers' Company in the City of London and carried out by Olivia O'Sullivan and Anne Thomas of the Centre for Language in Primary Education.

The project involved working with three London primary schools:

- Berger Primary School, Hackney
  The school has 14 classes, ages 5–11 (two-form entry), and a Nursery
- Gallions Mount Primary School, Greenwich
  The school has 14 classes, ages 5–11 (two-form entry), and a Nursery.
- St Luke's Church of England Primary School, Lambeth
  The school has 7 classes, ages 5–11 (one-form entry).

All of the schools were interested in developing their understanding of children's spelling development and in promoting effective teaching and learning strategies in the classroom.

There were two main strands to the project:

- an investigation into the teaching and learning of spelling from Reception to Year 6
- case studies of a small number of children in Years 4, 5 and 6 who read competently but were experiencing difficulties with spelling.

The context of the inquiry

Much research in the area of children's spelling has tended to focus on children as individuals in isolation from their progress as readers and writers in the classroom and school context, or it has focused primarily on children with difficulties – especially pupils of secondary age who have difficulties in spelling and/or reading. Our inquiry aimed to examine the cognitive aspects of children's development in spelling, and to do so in the living contexts of their many different classrooms, when they were working with teachers and alongside peers. We were also aware of the very important role played by their families.

Over the three years schools were visited twice per term for the first two years and once per term in year three. Additionally, staff meetings or inservice training days were held at least once per term in order to discuss current issues in spelling and the work of the project. Regular discussions were held with headteachers, English co-ordinators, and in one school the Special Needs co-ordinator, to review and plan the work of the project.

Research methods

Case studies

Thirty-one case study children were identified initially, from across the primary age range. In the second year, twelve of these children were selected for closer study while we continued to collect writing samples from all of the original 31 children. We talked with the main case study children about their writing and spelling development on each visit.

Writing samples

Approximately 2–3 writing samples (from a range of writing contexts) were collected each term from each case study child. Some of these were selected by teachers, but increasingly they were selected by the project team as we focused on particular features of children's development.

CLPE Spelling Assessment Framework

We analysed children's development using a diagnostic grid drawn from the work of Peters and Smith (1993). The CLPE Spelling Assessment Framework that we developed was a tool for analysing children's spelling development and their patterns of learning. The framework was invaluable, both as a framework for looking at development and as an inservice training tool for teachers. The framework is discussed both in Chapter 4, which discusses the case studies and in Chapter 6, 'Monitoring spelling'.

Reading samples

Throughout the project we discussed children's reading interests with them and their teachers. Reading samples were carried out with the principal case study children and these were tape recorded in the third year of the project.

Teacher interviews

Teacher interviews were carried out at the beginning of the project as part of developing an overview of their thinking about spelling and teaching approaches. A smaller group of teachers was interviewed in greater depth in the third year of the project.

Classroom observations

Regular classroom observations were carried out of teachers teaching, children learning and provision for spelling (e.g. the resources in the classroom and their use).

Questionnaire

A questionnaire, based on some draft guidelines for teaching spelling, was developed to help teachers reflect on their practice.

Staff meetings and inservice training

Staff meetings and inservice training were an important part of the project. We met with whole school staffs to discuss ideas about spelling development and teaching approaches, to present findings and to share key aspects of the project such as the CLPE Spelling Assessment Framework.

The case study data

In order to track children's spelling development over the three years of the project, 31 children were initially chosen as case studies, ten from two schools and eleven from the third. Over the three years a number of children from the case study group left the schools. If they were from the core group, they were replaced by a child from the broader group.

The case studies served a number of purposes in the project:

- to observe and collect evidence on the spelling development of a range of children between 5 and 11 years old on a longitudinal basis;
- to observe and collect evidence on individual children between 7 and 11 years old who were competent readers but who were experiencing difficulties with the spelling system; also included in this group were a few children experiencing both spelling and reading difficulties;
- to highlight any key issues in teaching and learning which arose in the course of the project.

The case study children came from a variety of socio-economic, cultural and linguistic backgrounds. Girls and boys were evenly represented in both case study groups.

Our research not only allowed us to consider the cognitive dimensions of spelling development in the primary age range but also raised our awareness of the range of experiences – both outside and within the school – which contributed to children's spelling knowledge.

Approximately one quarter of the original group of case study children were either from homes where English was not the dominant language, or from homes where languages additional to English were spoken; other children were English-speaking children, of whom eight were from African or Caribbean backgrounds. Many children attended community or religious schools, often for substantial periods. Quite often, in these settings, children encountered different models of literacy learning, such as in learning to read and write the Qu'ran. Because of its religious importance, this kind of teaching precludes experimentation and is based on learning the text by heart.

Although the spelling development of bilingual children was not a central focus of our project, we felt it important that this issue formed part of our discussion. During the project some of the bilingual case study children moved on. The remaining bilingual children were those for whom English was the dominant rather than an additional language.

Table 1.1 The case study children by gender, and by ethnicity and languages spoken at home

School	1	2	3	Total
Total case study children	10	11	10	31
Boys	4	7	3	14
Girls	6	4	7	17
African and Caribbean	0	4	4	8
Asian	4	0	0	4
English, Scottish and Welsh	5	6	3	14
European	1	1	1	3
Children from homes where languages other than English spoken	5	3	2	10

Data analysis

From the second year of the project the analysis of the case study data began. This involved analysis of all the pieces of writing collected from each main case study child over the year, using an analysis framework. Using the framework (see fig. 1.1), analysis was carried out under the following headings:

- Date of writing/child's age
- Kind of writing
- Observations: general
- Main strategies
- Developing competences
- Teacher strategies

This data provided information about the overall development of children's writing, and included information about spelling, handwriting and punctuation. The CLPE Spelling Assessment Framework (see Chapter 6) was used to analyse in detail children's developing spelling strategies. Further analysis of features of some children's writing, such as word length, was also carried out. For a full discussion of six case studies, see Chapter 5.

Effective teaching

As a result of our analysis of the case study data we arrived at conclusions about the most effective teaching approaches being used in the project schools. Conclusions and recommended teaching approaches based on these conclusions are in Chapter 6.

CLPE Case study analysis

Name Jonathan
Gender Boy   Languages English   DOB 9/6/88   School/School Year Y4

Date of writing/ child's age	Kind of writing	Observations: general	Main strategies / Developing competences	Teacher strategies
1 Beginning Autumn Term 1994	List. Instructions to slaves - presumably part of class topic	10-point list. Probably result of class discussion	Handwriting - a few words joined, capitals at beginning of some words. Approx 75 % of words spelled in standard form. Analysis of errors - phonetic attempts eg lachis - lashes or mostly just out by one letter eg oter (other), obay (obey), puse (push)	None evident
2 24.11.94	Very brief letter to a friend about a book he's read		Some high-frequency words spelled in standard form, others eg gose, littel , calld - phonetic attempts. With unknown words also uses phonetic strategies eg intogalactic (intergalactic), prehestorc (prehistoric) kichin (kitchen) Needs help in understanding common prefixes, suffixes	Three are underlined, possibly by teacher. Jonathan has written out 2 words at the end of the piece: control, circuits.
3 29.3.95	Account of class visit to Sainsbury's, probably preceded by class discussion.	A brief account which terminates rather abruptly. His own voice begins to come through in one or two personally observed details	Handwriting mostly joined. Full stops and capitals seem to be established. Most words spelled in standard form: some phonetic strategies - cept (kept), peopol (people), wrong letter pattern - saflie (safely) needs to focus on double consonants: geting (getting), shoping (shopping) caled (called) Spelling conference: 'If I can't spell a word I put it in my book and go and ask my teacher'. Uses a dictionary 'sometimes'.	None evident

Figure 1.1 Example of case study analysis

Chapter 2

Learning and teaching spelling

How do children learn to spell and how can teachers work most effectively to support their progress in spelling? The CLPE/Mercers Spelling Project focused on these two main questions. The evidence which most influenced our understanding of these questions came from observations of the case study children and interviews with them over a period of three years. The following brief snapshots of two children's development over that time highlight some of the main issues which arose from the case studies.

Shareen – a 'correct' speller

At the age of five Shareen wrote carefully, spelling each word in standard form.

Year 1, Term 1, 5 years 10 months
On Saturday I went to the school fair and on my way home I saw my mummy

At this stage Shareen was very reluctant to write unless she could make sure of the standard spelling of each word, either by asking adults or by referring to her personal word book. The presentation of her work – accurate spelling and very neat, well-controlled handwriting – reflected this sense of purpose, of the importance of getting things right. This unwillingness to take risks limited her writing. There was no possibility of assessing her spelling development as she relied totally on copying correct spellings.

Year 2, Term 1, 6 years 9 months
On Satday I went to the senmar. With my mum and my friend as wll and It was fany as wll. But it was good.

This piece of writing from the first term of Year 2 contained the very first signs of Shareen taking risks with spellings: e.g. *Satday* (Saturday), *senmar* (cinema), *fany* (funny) and *wll* (well). In fact these misspellings represented a minor breakthrough as far as Shareen's approach to learning spelling was concerned: she was now confident enough to draw upon her knowledge of the spelling system in order to hypothesise how some words might be spelt.

Year 2, Term 1, 6 years 11 months
One evng Juese and his disipolls was salln in a boat. . The boat began to roc baka and foth and the desaplls was rardu (worried). They acst Juese dut (don't) you cer (care).
(Extract)

This sample, also from the first term of Year 2, represents a more extended piece of writing: a story about Jesus and his disciples. Shareen had obviously enjoyed the story and in her retelling her focus was very definitely on composition rather than transcription. On this occasion she was less concerned with total accuracy in spelling – she was writing a first draft – whereas previously at whatever stage of writing, she would have relied almost entirely on using known words or on copying. Although at a first glance it may seem that in this piece Shareen's ability to spell had deteriorated from her work in Year 1, this extract shows that her knowledge of the system was

increasing. She was now engaging more actively in learning to spell and in thinking about unknown spellings.

The next example, from the third term of Year 2, shows Shareen drawing on her phonological knowledge of the links between sounds and letters as a way of encoding unfamiliar words. This was the approach that she began to adopt more frequently when she was not able to use known spellings.

Year 2, Term 3, 7 years 4 months

On Saturday my dad was going to cut the grass ... I asct (asked) can I help you dad yes but don't cut my best cholips (tulips) ... we staed (started) to cut the grass ... I codet (couldn't) cip (keep) a proms (promise) I cut the heds (heads) off ... my dad was furis (furious) ... I was very upset apte (about) it. (Extracts)

Shareen's preferred strategy as a speller over three years remained that of building up a substantial vocabulary of known spellings. On the one hand this strategy supported her writing development – through increasing her confidence – but on the other hand it may also have curbed her progress to some extent. Although she became somewhat more prepared to take risks (and therefore make errors) in her spelling, she was still inclined to limit much of what she said as a writer to words she knew how to spell.

Over the period of the case study, Shareen progressed from being a speller whose only concern was with correctness to someone who was prepared to take some risks, but who was over-reliant on the sounds of words as a guide to their spelling. It was possible to detect a notable gap between those words she knew how to spell and those that she didn't: her independent spellings were almost entirely reliant on phonetic strategies. Shareen's marked preference for a phonetic approach to spelling was supported by teaching at home. Shareen had yet to learn about analogy-making – using all that she knew about common letter strings and the appearance of familiar words to attempt the spelling of new words.

Shareen's case study raised a number of questions that were to recur throughout this project. How did her particular line of development relate to teachers' overall expectations of children's spelling progress during Key Stage 1? What kinds of teaching could help her make further progress? And how could she be led to look more carefully at the structures of words and spelling patterns? In general, how do children's individual learning styles seem to affect their progress in spelling? What kinds of teaching and classroom provision are most necessary if all children, whatever their initial strategies, are to become competent spellers? These are some of the issues that concerned and interested us as the project proceeded.

Stephen – a fluent reader at Key Stage 2 whose spelling did not match his reading

At the beginning of the project in Year 4, Stephen was a fairly confident and expressive writer, who wrote fairly rapidly. He had a vocabulary of words that he could spell but was nonetheless identified by his teacher as having a problem with spelling because his competence in spelling did not match his considerable fluency in reading. He enjoyed reading information books, particularly about the Greeks.

In the following piece, his misspellings showed in a number of instances that he was frequently only one or two letters 'out': e.g. *diffrent*, *colapsed* and *brack* (break). He also used a phonetic approach for some words, as in *yousing* (using).

Year 4, Term 1, 8 years 11 months

Then the merchant lost the dagger and Ares fount it. He loved it and he got all the gold he wanted. Then he lost it in the sea and a fish a men fount it. He was mad and he kept yousing it and lots and lots of diffrent colour lights. So it was easey to find it. The town had been destroyed and the roofs had colapsed. The only way to get it back to normal was to brack the dagger and the spell will brack ... (Extract)

Another piece, written later in Year 4, showed that with less familiar words Stephen frequently chose the 'wrong' spelling pattern – as in *weard* for *weird*. He seemed oblivious to structural features such as word endings (*-ite* in *favourite* and *-ion* in *religion*). Occasionally, Stephen still continued to use phonetic strategies, such as writing *togevar* for *together*.

Year 4, Term 2, 9 years 3 months

Henry VIII had blue eyes. He was fat because he ate to mutch. He wears a cloack, tunic, tites, a hat, rope belt and Julry. He was boold (bald) so his hat could fit him. He had these weard shoes like duck bekes. He had lots and lots of patons on his cloth's as he got older he got very ugly. He was very rich and his faverout ship was the marry rose. He had six wives. Henry VIII was a stubben man he liked plays and pageants. He was a nasty man and he killed two of his wives. He broke his religen by getting divorced. (Extract)

Why do some children (and adults) like Stephen, who are fluent readers, seem to find it difficult to use what they know already (as demonstrated in their correct spellings) in approaching a less familiar

word? Stephen's teacher at that time drew attention to his misspellings by writing the correct form either in the margin or at the end of the piece, but it was not clear how far Stephen was learning from these corrections. It seemed that simple corrections were not enough and that Stephen needed help in seeing how words were related, for example how *dig* changes to *digging* and *dug*. How could he have been encouraged to play a more active role in his own spelling development? What other teaching approaches would have been helpful in enabling him to move forward?

Year 5, Term 3, 10 years 4 months

One day along time ago Odysseus a worrer was going back to Greece on a ship with the rest of his army ... While Midas was listning to pans music Appollow came to listion as well he thourt that Pan's music was better than hes owne so Appollow siad "I challenge pan to a duel of musis." "O.K." and Mount Tmolus is the place were we duel ... Appollow was so mad with minas that he gave him donkey ears. when Minas go home he got a wig to cover his ears and the only one who know about minases big ears was his barber. (Extract)

In this extract, written a year later in the summer term of Y5, Stephen seemed to be taking fewer risks in his writing – thus resulting perhaps in a slightly lower rate of misspellings than in Year 4. Despite a growing vocabulary of known words, there were continuing errors associated especially with the visual aspects of spelling and with word structures. His miscues were often recognisable letter strings – such as *ion* in *listion* (listen) or *llow* in *Appollo* – but were used inappropriately and reveal that in Year 5 Stephen still had far to go before he was fully in control of the spelling system.

Why given that Stephen was a fluent reader, could he not use more of the knowledge gained from reading to inform his spelling? How could teachers have supported Stephen's development further, and to what extent could Stephen have been helped to help himself? How might a careful analysis of Stephen's spelling errors have helped his teachers to help him? These were questions which began to arise during the project and to which we began to search for answers.

Teaching spelling

At the beginning of the project there were a number of issues arising from our observations of school and classroom practice:

- Approaches in the three schools varied but in all cases there was not enough emphasis at the beginning of the project on the teaching of spelling. In one school there was over-reliance on a scheme with not enough analysis of children's spelling development, while in another there was good practice in the teaching of writing but not enough emphasis on helping children's spelling development within their writing. The third school had a more eclectic overall approach.
- Approaches were very different between classes and teachers within the same school, for example in the way teachers intervened to support children's spelling at the early stages or marked and responded to children's work.
- There was little active teaching of spelling as part of classroom practice, e.g. word study approaches were infrequently observed.
- Resources for spelling and their use varied considerably between classes. Even where resources existed, teachers did not always integrate them into practice through encouraging children to use them and showing them how.
- Overall there was a need for development in the area of spelling through teacher INSET with a pulling together of approaches; individually teachers had many excellent strategies.
- Schools referred to parents' concerns but there was no guidance from schools for parents.

At the beginning of the project, it also became apparent that many teachers felt unsure about how to teach spelling in a constructive way. Some were concerned about inhibiting children's writing by focusing too closely on their spelling. They tended to see teaching spelling mainly as a question of correcting errors, rather than a way of developing an interest in, and attention to, words and their structures. Throughout discussions with the case study children, classroom observations and discussions with teachers, we began to consider the following questions:

- What role does the teaching of writing play in the teaching of spelling?
- What role does the teaching and learning of reading play in learning to spell?
- How can spelling be taught effectively in whole class or group contexts?
- What elements would form the basis of a programme for teaching spelling in the Early Years and at Key Stages 1 and 2?
- What provision and resources are needed to support spelling development at different stages?
- What issues need to be considered in helping children learning to spell in English as an additional language?
- How can teachers intervene to support individual children's spelling without undermining their confidence and willingness to take risks, particularly in the early stages?
- Do children having difficulties in spelling need special kinds of teaching and provision?
- How can teachers be helped to analyse children's spelling development? And how can such assessments be used as a basis for teaching and moving children on?

This chapter has raised some of the main theoretical and pedagogical issues in the learning and teaching of spelling that arose from the case studies. In the following chapters we present some of the findings of the project's work with schools, teachers and children, as well as practical guidance for teachers and schools.

Chapter 3

Understanding spelling

Learning to spell has frequently been a subject of controversy particularly with regard to the way it is taught in schools. As a result of conflicting arguments over the last decade, together with the high media profile given to spelling and reading, there is often confusion and uncertainty about teaching spelling, both amongst teachers and in society at large. To understand how spelling works in English and how it can be taught most effectively, we need to consider English spelling in a historical perspective. If we then examine the different influences on the teaching of spelling over the past few decades, we can develop a more coherent picture both of this surprisingly complex topic and of the different kinds of knowledge that children need in order to become effective spellers. There is no doubt that teachers have a central role to play in this process.

The development of English spelling

Throughout the history of Britain, it is common knowledge that the English language has been subject to a very wide range of influences as a result of different contacts, conquests and periods of occupation. The influence of languages such as Latin, Greek, Saxon, Scandinavian languages and Norman French, is still very much in evidence in contemporary English spelling (for fuller accounts see Henderson, 1990; Temple *et al.* 1988; Torbe, 1995; Mudd, 1994). Later, a further influence on the spelling of English was the employment of Dutch and German print workers in the production of printed books. Standard English spelling is of course a relatively recent innovation (it began with the arrival of the printing press and was fixed with the introduction of the dictionary) and even now is subject to changing fashions and preferences. Furthermore, as with all languages, the English language and its spelling are constantly evolving, and are now open to other influences from forms of English spoken in other parts of the world.

For all of these reasons, spelling in English is a complicated business and it cannot be argued that the spelling system is an optimal one, or an easy one for a young learner to come to terms with. This complex system also affects children learning to read: some have argued that children take longer to learn to read in English than in other European languages with more regular and predictable spelling systems (Stubbs, 1980). Researchers, theorists and educators have often grappled with these considerations in an attempt to understand how children can be taught effectively. Here we consider some of the theoretical contributions which have been most significant in developing a modern pedagogy.

Spelling as a perceptual process

For much of the twentieth century spelling has been seen mainly as a process involving visual and auditory processing. The work of Fred Schonell and particularly his book *Essentials in Teaching and Testing Spelling* (1932), which was based on his research into spelling disability, was dominant both in the field of theory and in school practice. Schonell's spelling lists divided words into graded groups according to perceived patterns (both auditory and visual), but were in many ways totally arbitrary. These word lists related to adult vocabulary and took no account of the words most frequently used by children. They were initially intended mainly for use as an assessment tool. However, the lists were subsequently came to dominate what was taught in schools and still continue to contribute heavily to current misunderstandings about teaching and learning spelling

– that it is mainly about rote learning and that, in learning to spell, correctness is the paramount consideration.

This approach to teaching also had the effect of separating the teaching of spelling from the process of writing. A decade later, Grace Fernald (1943) developed these ideas further. She emphasised the importance of working with the words arising in children's own writing as a basis for development and the role of kinaesthetic training (through tracing and handwriting) in learning letter patterns.

Spelling caught or taught?

One of the major debates in the first half of the century had been whether spelling is 'caught' incidentally from reading and writing or whether it needs to be taught systematically A crucial influence on thinking in this area came from the work of Margaret Peters (*Spelling Caught or Taught*, 1985), who challenged the idea that spelling is caught mainly from reading. She argued that children who have not begun to 'catch' the system by the time they are seven years old need systematic teaching.

Peters maintained that visual recall of words is the crucial factor in spelling development and that this is best achieved through systematic attention to letter patterns and to the serial probability of letters in English. She considered that the turning point in children's spelling development is when they begin to move away from a total reliance on translating sounds into symbols and become more aware of the visual dimensions of the English spelling system. She pointed out that children's attention should be drawn not only to words which sound alike and look alike, but also – and very importantly – to words which look alike and do not sound alike, e.g. *one, done, gone, bone*. She advocated that children should learn to spell by being taught to look at words with 'interest, intent and intention' to reproduce a word.

Peters thought that handwriting teaching, particularly through the practice of letter patterns, could play a significant role in children's spelling development, through establishing fluency, legibility and speed. Many of these ideas were taken up in schools through the influential publications and research of Charles Cripps, who worked closely with Margaret Peters. Peters and Cripps advocated the Look–Cover–Write–Check strategy as an essential approach to learning new words. This strategy was based on the idea of visual recall in spelling:

1   LOOK at the word carefully and in such a way that you will remember what you have seen.
2   COVER the word so you cannot see it.
3   WRITE the word from memory, saying it softly to yourself as you are writing.
4   CHECK what you have written. If you have not written the word correctly do not alter it, instead go back and repeat all these steps again.

Charles Cripps further developed the link between handwriting teaching and children's learning of spelling (Cripps and Cox, 1990). He suggested that the early development of a fluent handwriting style, preferably joined, would facilitate an awareness of the visual patterning of the spelling system (i.e., common letter strings). Cripps' and Peters' work continues to be an important influence on practice in teaching spelling, but is of more value at KS2 than in the early years of learning to spell.

Spelling in the writing process

In the 1960s and 70s, particularly in North America, sociolinguists and psycholinguists began to draw parallels between the way children acquired spoken language and the way in which they developed as readers (Slobin, 1971; Goodman, 1982; Smith, 1982). Aspects of language and literacy development were no longer being considered in isolation from one another and this generated new ways of thinking about the way in which children learned to write. Learning written language was increasingly seen as learning a new function of language, and not simply as the transmission of a set of skills to be learned in sequence.

In the 1980s there was a further major shift in thinking about children's development as writers. Spelling had up until this time usually been considered rather in isolation from the writing process, and there was a marked reluctance in schools to allow childen to write before they could spell – young children often 'wrote' by copying under teachers' writing. Frank Smith (1982) offered a fundamental insight into writing when he described the process as consisting of two discrete but interrelated parts: composition and transcription.

COMPOSITION (author)	TRANSCRIPTION (secretary)
Getting ideas	Physical effort of writing
Selecting ideas	Spelling
Grammar	Capitalisation
	Punctuation
	Paragraphs
	Legibility

This model saw the development of secretarial skills (e.g. spelling and handwriting) as separate from the authorial dimensions of writing. Smith argued that young children can compose (have ideas and put them into words) before they learn to spell. About inventive spelling, he was realistic: 'Learning to spell takes time; it begins with misspelling.' Smith suggested that 'Children who write only the words they know how to spell end up writing (and knowing how to spell) very few words indeed'.

Smith's emphasis on the value of children writing independently from early on was part of a general move towards encouraging children to see themselves as writers from the beginning of schooling. To use the words of the Russian psychologist Vygotsky, the focus in teaching writing in the infants school began to shift from 'the mechanics of writing' and from teaching writing as a 'complicated motor skill' to seeing writing as a 'turning point in the entire cultural development of the child' (Vygotsky, 1978).

Smith's model of writing influenced the Primary Language Record, which considered writing under the two headings of composition and transcription, and the first English National Curriculum which, drawing heavily on the wording of the *Primary Language Record Handbook* (1988), created separate attainment targets for Writing, Spelling and Punctuation.

Spelling and cognitive development

During the same period, psychologists and researchers began to take a great interest in children's early development as writers and in the ways in which children 'came to know' about aspects of the writing system. Ferreiro and Teberosky (1979) carried out a major study of pre-school children from a range of social backgrounds in Buenos Aires, Argentina. What they found was that, even before formal schooling, children were actively involved in constructing hypotheses about written language. Ferreiro and Teberosky put forward the view that 'writing is a conceptual task, as well as a psycho-motor task' and that development therefore 'is not passive copying but active interpretations of the models of the adult world'. Their research led them to identify discernible patterns of progression in children's development as readers and spellers which could be clearly linked to Piagetian theory.

Following on from the work of Ferreiro and Teberosky studies were undertaken by academic researchers who were also parents of their own young children at home. Glenda Bissex (1980) and Shirley Payton (1984) highlighted significant factors in children's writing and spelling development. Glenda Bissex's son wrote before he could read, and therefore before he was aware that written words have standard spellings. His early spellings were made up of a predominance of consonants, a minimal use of vowels, and a use of letter-name spellings (e.g. 'R U DF' for 'Are you deaf?'), all of which reflected the fact that he was making hypotheses about the relationships between speech sounds and letters. Bissex called her book 'GNYS AT WRK' (Genius at work), which was a sign her son had pinned to his bedroom door.

As Paul Bissex's competence in spelling began to grow, due to his increasing experience of reading and writing, he gradually introduced more vowels into his writing and his invented spellings became increasingly thoughtful. By the age of eight, the primary areas of growth were in the 'visual (recall) and semantic (morphemic) strategies within his expanded understanding of the nature of our spelling system' (Bissex 1980, p. 195).

Paul Bissex's spelling of 'directions'	
DRAKTHENS	(5.7)
DRAKSHINS	(5.8)
DIRECKSHONS	(7.5)
DIREKSHONS	(7.5)
DIRECTIONS but not sure if the ending was OI or IO	(8.1)
DIRECTIONS without question	(8.7)

Spelling as a developmental process

A number of American researchers now turned their attention in particular to children's spelling progress viewed as a developmental process (Temple *et al.*, 1982; Henderson, 1984; Gentry, 1987). These researchers identified progressions in children's invented spelling which formed a developmental sequence, moving in stages from children's earliest attempts to symbolise words towards standard spellings. There were slight differences in emphasis and interpretation but these models were essentially similar. Particularly influential in the UK has been the work of Gentry who sees children's spelling as falling into five developmental stages:

1   *Precommunicative.* Spellers randomly string together letters of the alphabet without regard to letter-sound correspondence. Example: OPSPO = eagle; RTAT = eighty
2   *Semiphonetic.* Letters represent sounds but only some of the sounds are represented. Example: E = eagle; A = eighty
3   *Phonetic.* Words are spelled like they sound. The speller represents all of the phonemes within a word though spellings may be unconventional. Example: EGL = eagle; ATE = eighty
4   *Transitional.* A visual memory of spelling patterns is apparent. Spellings exhibit conventions of English orthography vowels in every syllable, e-marker and vowel digraph patterns, correctly spelled inflectional endings, and frequent English letter sequences. Example EGUL = eagle; EIGHTEE = eighty
5   *Correct.* The word is spelled correctly (Gentry 1991).

Gentry's developmental sequence, as well as showing what children knew about spelling, offered a means of assessing children's development in this area by analysing their misspellings and also, potentially, offered areas of focus for teaching.

Gentry's model, and others like it, influenced pedagogy both in the USA and in the UK. But this close focus on developmental stages gave rise to a number of unfortunate consequences. The evidence of a developmental sequence in spelling was so strong that a tendency developed among many teachers and educationalists to see progression as occurring almost independently of adult intervention. During the early 1980s, the 'developmental' or 'emergent' writing movement appeared, in its most extreme form, to be advocating learning by discovery with little or no role for the teacher except to encourage children to 'have a go' at spellings.

Linked to this was an over-emphasis on the phonetic aspects of invented spelling, at the expense of helping children to take on the visual aspects of English spelling (although this transitional stage is a crucial

part of Gentry's developmental model). A fascination with children's early and original spellings dominated discussion. There was a need for a broader view of learning to spell and a clearer understanding of the range of strategies that children need in order to become competent spellers. There unquestionably *is* a basic developmental dimension to children's progress in spelling, but children always need information, support and teaching to help them move on in their learning. The hard question is always how this teaching can be provided most effectively, so that it connects with children's understandings.

Spelling, reading and phonological awareness

It will be plain from all that has gone before that children's learning to spell is closely related to their understandings of how spoken language is written down, and thus to their learning to read. One of the central questions posed by linguists and psychologists alike, most recently during the 1980s, has been the nature of the relationship between children's reading and spelling development. In the most basic definition, reading seems to be concerned with *decoding* written language, while writing and spelling seem to be concerned mainly with *encoding* or generating written language.

Because spelling focuses on the way in which sounds are encoded, it can be seen as the other side of phonics; children who are learning to spell are learning a great deal about sound–letter relationships. To spell phonetically, which is for most of them (as Gentry suggests) an early strategy, children need to analyse the sounds they hear in words and work out how to represent them. They are greatly helped in this by their developing 'phonological awareness' (their awareness of the sounds of language) and their 'phonemic awareness' (their awareness of the smallest units of sound). For many young children who are writing independently writing and spelling may well be the sites where they can learn sound–letter correspondences most effectively, at the point where they most need to make use of them. Therefore, any discussion of learning to spell also needs to take into account recent research into learning to read.

The development of children's phonological awareness is one important recent area of research in reading and there are implications in this work for thinking about spelling. Phonological awareness, which is developed from birth onwards, is a broad term describing the ability to register, rehearse and categorise, albeit at a pre-conscious level, the sounds of a language. Children's early play with language and rhyme is an important part of this development.

The work of Bradley and Bryant drew attention to the way in which children's early competence in detecting rhyming words predicted their later reading competence (Bryant and Bradley, 1985). Usha Goswami pursued this line of thought further in her research into the effect of phonological awareness on children's subsequent literacy development (Goswami and Bryant, 1991; Goswami, 1995). She argues that there are three levels or stages of phonological awareness at a within-word level: an awareness of syllables; an awareness of onset and rime; an awareness of phonemes. This sequence holds true for all alphabetic languages where studies have been done (Goswami, 1999).

An awareness of syllables is seen as being founded on children's ready response to the rhythm of words; later, an understanding of syllabification comes to play an important role in children's spelling development (e.g. by enabling them to segment a word like 'tea-cher').

1   *Syllables*
    bath + room = bathroom
    Sat + ur + day = Saturday

2   *Onset and rime*
    (Onset: the part of the syllable before the first vowel.
    Rime: the part of the syllable from the first vowel onwards.)

Onset		Rime	
s	+	ing	= sing
st	+	ing	= sting
str	+	ing	= string

3   *Phonemes*
    (Phonemes: the smallest units of sounds)
    s + a + n + d = sand
    h + a + ll = hall
    sh + o + p = shop

Onset and rime

Goswami's research, which refers more to the reading than the spelling process but which has strong implications for the teaching of spelling, suggests that onsets (the *s-* in *sing*, the *st-* in *sting* and the *str-* in *string*) and rimes (the *-ing* in *sing*, *sting* and *string*) provide a fundamental insight for children into the links between how words are said and how they are written down. Learning to split words into onsets and rimes is relatively easy for children and provides the basis for a more consciously analytic approach to language. Rime is the element of consistency which allows children to begin to see relationships between some groups of words, rather than seeing each word as an individual unit.

In addition, dividing words into onset and rime helps to sort out one of the major problems in reading: the pronunciation of vowels. Vowels are the most unpredictable element in the English spelling system and the major reason why 'sounding words out' is not an easily workable strategy in English. But whereas 'a' sounds different in *ball*, *bathe*, *bar*, *bare* and *bat*, it sounds the same in *ball*, *hall*, *call*, and *fall*; that is, in words that share the same rime. A focus on rime makes vowels less ambiguous for children either in reading or in spelling.

Goswami found that for most children an awareness of syllables and onsets and rimes in speech develops *before* an awareness of phonemes (the smallest units of sound). She demonstrated that for young children the phonemes that are easier to detect *in speech* are those at the beginning of words which correspond to single-consonant onsets (e.g. *b* in *b-at*, *s* in *s-ing*, *t* in *t-en*). She pointed out that phonemes embedded in longer onsets (e.g. the *t* in *str*) are more difficult to identify, as are phonemes which are embedded in rimes (e.g. the *n* in *sand*). It seems to be for these reasons that children draw on initial letter sounds, the predominant phonemes in words, in their early writing. In Chapter 3 we will argue at more length that it is likely that phonemic awareness develops in spelling rather than in reading.

Making analogies

Perhaps the most significant aspect of Goswami's work points to children's ability not only to identify onsets and rimes but also to make analogies between words they know how to spell and unfamiliar words with the same rime (e.g. *dog* and *fog*, *hand* and *grand*). Recognising and making analogies between words with the same rime helps children to begin to classify groups of words (in this case, those that contain the same phonological patterns) and so build up a significant spelling repertoire. As children's reading vocabulary increases, they are able to draw on more examples and make more analogies, in reading and also in spelling. Later, analogy continues to be among the most important tools that children can draw on to analyse and recall spelling patterns.

However, to restrict discussion of spelling development to its phonological aspects and to neglect visual, structural and semantic aspects would be misleading; any theory of how reading and spelling interconnect needs to look at how the written language reflects not only the sounds of words but also their syntactical structures and their meanings.

The relationship between reading and writing development

In order to establish whether decoding (reading) and encoding (writing) are two sides of the same process or two distinct processes, researchers and educationists have tended to focus either on what is similar about reading and spelling processes or what is dissimilar, according to their particular discipline. But the relationship between reading and spelling may not be a constant one. At different points in children's learning, they may be attending to different aspects of written language and using different strategies.

Uta Frith is an influential psychologist who has fundamentally influenced thinking about the relationship between reading and spelling development. Her model of development (Frith, 1985) analysed children's development into three overlapping phases: logographic, alphabetic and orthographic. She described children as learning to be able to:

- recognise whole words in context (logographic phase);
- analyse within-word units e.g. onsets and rimes, phonemes (alphabetic or analytic phase);
- read or spell words fluently 'without reference to phonological conversion' (orthographic phase).

In essence, what Frith describes is a movement from whole words to parts of words and back to an attention to whole-word structures (cf. Henrietta Dombey, *Whole-to-part Phonics*, CLPE 1998). Each of these three phases, according to Frith 'is divided into two steps with either reading or writing as the pacemaker of the strategy which identifies the phase'. Frith thus mapped the interplay between children's development as 'decoders' and 'encoders'.

The six-step model of skills in reading and writing acquisition

Frith's model (Fig. 3.2) indicates precisely this point. She indicates, for example, that children's growing ability to analyse within-word units (e.g. phonemes, onsets) precedes their ability to do so in their reading. Later on their fluent orthographic reading precedes similar development in spelling.

Frith's model also suggests where the emphasis of teaching needs to be in order to support these developing understandings, not only in the early stages of learning the code, but also in the later (orthographic) stages when children are extending their repertoire as spellers and learning to look carefully at letter patterns and word structures. In her later work Frith draws upon this model to consider the relationship between reading and spelling with regard to children who are (a) good readers and good spellers, (b) good readers and poor spellers, and (c) poor readers and poor spellers. (For further discussion of this point see Chapter 5, Part 2.)

Ehri (1979) also hypothesised that learning to read and learning to spell were systematically related. Significantly, Ehri maintained that the ways in which children remember how words are spelled are linked not only to the 'phonological identities' of words but also to their 'syntactic and semantic' identities. In other words, young competent spellers are able to distinguish which spelling goes with which meaning.

Spelling, meaning and the structure of words

Other researchers and educationists such as Henderson (1990) and Ramsden (1993) have pointed to the importance of seeing learning to spell as a process of linguistic development in which the meaning and structure of words become increasingly significant. Henderson saw development in three stages:

- Alphabet principle (using mainly consonants and letter names);
- Pattern principle (using common rimes and other letter patterns in spelling);
- Pattern by meaning principle (the stage where meaning plays the 'dominant role in spelling').

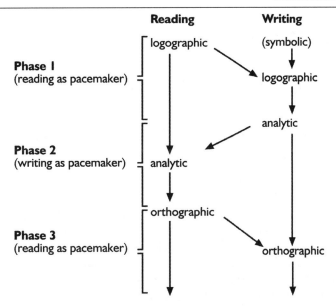

Figure 3.2   Frith's model of reading and writing development

Henderson made the point that helping children to become familiar with common letter patterns (both common rimes and visual letter patterns) helps to prepare them for the link between the spellings and meanings of words. For example, *ed* at the end of a word can be pronounced as *ed, id, t, ud, d*, depending on accent, stress and the word concerned: wanted (*wantid/wantud*), walked (*walkt*), spelled (*spelld*). Children come to know that, however the word is pronounced, the written ending (or suffix) remains constant in nearly all cases as *-ed*; meaning and pattern take precedence over sound in order to achieve this consistent spelling. Henderson argued that learning to spell was an active and concrete process, not a passive and abstract one. He also maintained strongly that

> word knowledge derives from reading and from applying the knowledge through purposeful writing. Spelling is thus pivotal to both reading and writing; in this sense it is central to the meaning and acquisition of literacy.
>
> Henderson and Templeton (1991)

Melvyn Ramsden develops this idea further in his book *Rescuing Spelling* (1993), where he argues that 'the English system of spelling principally represents meaning' (p. 23). While Henderson stressed the importance of structure in order to make the link between structure and meaning, Ramsden argues that morphemes, or units of meaning within words, are the principal way of helping children move from meaning to structure. Ramsden's book is principally a book about teaching, aimed particularly at teachers in the upper primary school and early secondary school. Like Henderson, he keenly advocates the teaching of word structures, roots and origins (etymology) through systematic word study activities.

Conclusion

In this chapter we have considered the work of some of the significant theorists and practitioners involved in thinking about children's spelling development and have traced their influence on teaching and learning over the past sixty years. We are now in a better position to reflect upon many of these ideas in relation to the work and findings of the CLPE/Mercers spelling project. While many of the theories discussed in this chapter influenced the thinking in this book, we also felt (based on extensive experience of children as language learners) that becoming a speller was most likely to be a multi-faceted process involving many different kinds of knowledge, and that children were likely to be different in their learning of spelling. It was the work in project schools over a three-year period, with the case study children and their teachers, that allowed us to develop and refine these understandings.

Chapter 4

Learning to spell

Stages of development or multiple sources of knowledge?

In the last chapter, we saw that since the 1980s there has been widespread acceptance of the view that children's spelling development falls into identifiable stages: that children move from pre-literate scribbles, to use of phonetic strategies, then through a transitional 'stage' where visual and structural aspects become more dominant before standard spelling is firmly established (Gentry, 1991; Read, 1986; Temple *et al.*, 1988). However, it seems clear from our research and the research of others (Lennox and Siegal, 1994; Snowling, 1994; Ellis, 1994; Treiman, 1994) that while learning to spell can be seen as a developmental process in that children move towards standard spelling more or less rapidly, always depending on their experiences and teaching, the 'stages' within this process are far from being invariable or discrete.

Samantha (5 years 8 months) wrote:

> To Mr Gumpy
> (words provided by teacher on flip chart)
> Sorry for hoppg anbt
> Thak you for litg me come
> on your doat
> Love from
> (words provided by teacher on flip chart)
> the ribbt
> *(Dear Mr Gumpy, Sorry for hopping about, thank you for letting me come on your boat. Love from the rabbit.)*

In this short piece of writing Samantha used the following strategies:

- she copied some words, e.g. *Mr Gumpy*;
- she knew some words by heart, e.g. *for, you, me, come*;
- she used phonetic strategies, e.g. *thak* (thank);
- she used visual strategies, e.g. the *oa* in *doat* (boat), the *pp* in *hoppg*;
- she may have been beginning to make analogies, e.g. *hoppg* (hopping) and *litg* (letting).

The case studies showed us that, rather than spelling development passing through discrete stages, what actually took place was that children began to draw on different sources of knowledge, even from the early stages. Early strategies developed, were added to and transformed as different kinds of knowledge developed and worked in reciprocal ways. As new strategies were added they could be seen operating at the same time as earlier strategies within a piece of writing.

> Learning to spell involves the integration of several skills. These include knowledge of phonological representations, grammatical and semantic knowledge, as well as the formulation of analogies with words in visual memory and the knowledge of orthographic rules and conventions.
>
> (Lennox and Siegel, 1994)

What different kinds of knowledge are involved in spelling?

The case studies demonstrated that it was important to consider children's spelling development in the context of their literacy development as a whole. In this chapter we therefore consider initially the broader effects of children's reading and writing on their spelling development, before going on to discuss categories of knowledge more particularly related to spelling.

Knowledge acquired from reading

What is the influence of reading on children's spelling development? This was one of the main questions which our inquiry set out to address – not only with regard to children at the early stages of schooling but also in relation to older children some of whom were experiencing spelling difficulties.

Through opportunities to engage with a wide range of texts children gained experience of language structures at many levels – semantic, syntactic and grapho-phonic. In these ways – not just at the level of word analysis – reading provided children with an ever-increasing store of implicit knowledge about written language.

Our case studies showed that all the children who were early competent spellers were also competent readers. In the main good spellers were children who took an enormous interest in all aspects of language and literacy. These children enjoyed reading, read a wide range of books at home and at school and saw their reading as a source of learning about vocabulary and spelling. They also seemed to take an active interest in how writers write, how they put words together (syntax), and in word meanings and spellings. In addition they were able to make generalisations from their observations of the nature of English spelling.

Eliot, one of our case study children, was an early competent reader and speller whose spellings were almost entirely in standard form at the beginning of Year 3. He was described by his teacher in Year 3 as 'able to handle more difficult novels' such as *Hope Leaves Jamaica* (Kate Elizabeth Ernest). Later he described how he had favourite authors – Roald Dahl and Robert Leeson. He was interested in information books 'especially about Roman times', and 'read for an hour a day at home'. He seemed to be able to make connections at many levels about spelling as a system and to be able to reflect on his learning explicitly

At the age of 8 (Year 3), Morgan, another of the case study children who was an early competent reader and speller, told us that she 'liked to write down difficult words in a little book and find out their meaning' and that she could 'read words like *amazement* and *hedgehog* and spell them'. Her favourite authors at this time were Anne Fine and Jan Mark.

The reverse of this generalisation was not universally true, however: some of our case study children were experienced readers and poor spellers. Not all children made connections between what they saw in print and how they went about reproducing words in writing. To a greater or lesser extent, these children saw the spelling system as arbitrary. This was true of children who were experienced readers and poor spellers but was even more so with regard to children who had difficulties both in reading and spelling.

Anna, aged 11 years 3 months, was an experienced reader who had difficulties with spelling. By Year 6, supported and encouraged by her teacher, there were major developments in her spelling. This took place in the context of her growth as both a reader and a writer. Her reading provided a model for her writing at all levels:

> I like writing stories. When I was at home it took me five pages to write (about) this girl going around the corner to the shop. Five pages for her just arriving at this shop and I had to read it to everyone! I'd read this book *William in Love* by Jean Ure. It's a brilliant book! So I wrote – I'm still writing – and I'm on my seventh page – and mine's called *Kate in Love*.

Knowledge acquired from writing

The children in the project who made most progress in spelling were those who had a wide range of opportunities to write, who wrote at length and who were helped by their teachers to become enthusiastic and committed writers. Our analysis of the case study children's texts showed that, as their texts got longer, the percentage of their misspellings declined and their attempts at unknown words improved.

For example, Samantha, in Reception and Year 1, was an avid writer who was given the opportunity by her teachers to write in a wide range of forms for different purposes. She used writing as part of her learning, from the earliest stages (Fig. 4.1), in both teacher-directed and self-initiated contexts. Fig. 4.2 shows some of the different kinds of writing she experienced during her Reception year and Year 1. The importance of opportunities to write applied both to young children at the early stages of writing and also to older inexperienced writers and spellers who were encountering difficulties with spelling. Christopher, who had experienced difficulties with spelling, made real progress as a writer and a speller in Years 5 and 6. He was encouraged to write in a gradually increasing range of forms (Fig. 4.3).

In addition, some of the case study children demonstrated, from early on, ways in which they had internalised the linguistic features of written genres:

Samantha (6yrs 5mths) wrote:
> One morning as the sun came up …
> (story narrative)

Lydia (6yrs 8mths) wrote:
> Ladybirds are good insects because they eat greenflies.
> (information text)

Eliot (Year 3) wrote:
> I looked at our raft with pride. There was no doubt that we would win the race.

These children were beginning to write with a reader's expectations in mind. There is no doubt that consistent and extensive opportunities to write played a decisive role in their development. These fluent writers had the experience of engaging with the spelling system in a problem-solving way through using a varied and widening vocabulary in their writing.

To summarise, our case studies showed:

- Rather than passing through discrete 'stages' of spelling development, children drew on multiple sources of knowledge from very early on, although individuals tended to favour particular strategies.
- Children did gain a good deal of implicit knowledge about spelling from their reading. But whereas some took an active interest in the meanings and spellings of words and were able to draw on their stored knowledge to make generalisations and analogies, not all children made these connections. Some tended to see the spelling system as arbitrary.
- Children who made the most progress in spelling were those who had a wide range of opportunities to write, and to write at length.

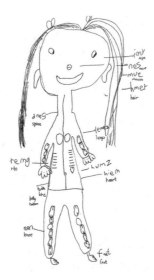

Figure 4.1 Diagram of the body, Samantha, 5 years 5 months

Samantha: kinds of writing collected in Reception year	Samantha: kinds of writing collected in Year 1
Personal narratives	Lists
Responses to texts	Prayers
Autobiography	Personal narratives
Lists	Timelines
Letters	Historical accounts
Labelled drawings	Creation stories
Scientific diagrams	More extended stories
Maps of the classroom and locality	Story maps
Story maps	Book making and publishing
Maths estimations	Information writing
Story narratives based on well known books	Autobiography
Book making and publishing	Copying out stories from books

Figure 4.2

Christopher: Kinds of writing collected in Years 5 and 6	
Story narratives	Historical accounts
Persuasive writing	Responses to scientific questions
Retellings of myths	Devising scientific definitions
Scientific accounts	Book reviews
Labelled diagrams	Diaries
Story/play plans	
Letters	
Posters	
Self-assessment accounts	

Figure 4.3

Specific categories of knowledge

In addition to drawing on general sources of knowledge from reading and writing, children also draw on specific kinds of knowledge in learning to spell. These specific categories of knowledge are detailed in the pages that follow.

1   Phonological knowledge

Many young children are aware that spelling involves 'drawing speech' and try to reproduce the sounds of words from early on. They are helped in this by their growing 'phonological awareness'. As discussed in the previous chapter, phonological awareness can be described as a growing awareness of the sounds of words, and of the various ways in which words can be split up, e.g. into syllables, onsets and rimes, phonemes (Goswami and Bryant, 1991; Goswami, 1995). Their developing knowledge is acquired initially at an aural level and becomes a significant building block in learning how language is written down. This broader concept of *phonological* knowledge is often narrowed down in discussions of reading, to a more restricted concept of phonemic knowledge – knowledge of sound–letter relationships.

Current discussions about literacy development tend to equate the way that phonological aware-ness is applied by children in reading and spelling, but it seems likely that there are significant differ-ences. Our case studies gave us detailed information about children's developing phonological and phonemic knowledge as it was revealed in their spelling. Particularly at the earlier stages, there seem to be a number of interlinked developments. First many children, although not all, used a phonemic approach as a first, spontaneous spelling strategy in their early spellings. For example, Jason wrote:

I P W M F E (I played with my fire engine).

and Dominic wrote

JK (Jack)

At this stage Jason and Dominic were clearly identifying the salient phonemes in words – many of which were also onsets (initial sounds). Treiman has pointed out that initial consonants in words are 'consistent in spelling-sound correspondence across about 96% of words' (for example *c* in *cat*, *c* in *car*) and that 'final consonants are consistent across about 91% of words' (for example, *p* in *soup*, *p* in *cup*)' (Treiman *et al.*, 1995). This consistency, and the fact that these consonants are easier to identify aurally because they are at the beginnings and ends of words, clearly accounts for many children's recourse to a phonemic strategy in their early spellings; this is an effective strategy. At this early stage, children's ability to segment words at a phonemic level may be more apparent in their spelling than in their reading. As Goswami and Bryant(1990, p. 148) pointed out, 'it is still not clear why children are so willing to break up words into phonemes when they write, and yet are so reluctant to think in terms of phonemes when they read'.

Phonological knowledge, and an awareness of how words can be segmented, assumes more importance in relation to vowels and their spellings. Treiman points out that vowels do not consistently represent the same sounds. 'Consistency of vowels stands at 51% across different words' (for example, the letter *a* makes a different sound in *cat, call, car, cake*; the digraph *ou* in *soup, loud, four*). However, when the entire rime is considered, vowel consistency increases to 77%. As Henrietta Dombey (Dombey *et al.*, 1998) points out, in reading English 'vowels are the problem' – and this is true for spelling just as much as reading. Children who are encouraged to hear and see the similarities between words with similar rimes are therefore learning an important strategy for spelling as well as for reading.

Dominic (in Year 2) for example used the following spellings:

nite	for	*night*
tort	for	*taught*
grane	for	*grain*

His choices show not only his preferred 'phonetic' approach in his analogy-making, but also a developing sense of plausible letter strings and of possible rimes. As children move on from an initial phonemic strategy to spelling in 'chunks', they may initially be influenced either by phonological hypotheses or in some cases by visual hypotheses.

But because the case study children were generally writing in a wide range of genres from the beginning, and because even in a short piece of meaningful writing there is virtually no possibility of writing only phonically 'regular' words, children's spelling was therefore not restricted to 'straightforward' phonological mapping. Instead we found that they knew about many different letter patterns and word structures from quite early on, and were able to make a wider range of choices.

Phonics in reading and spelling

Spelling and reading are not identical processes – if a child can read a word then he/she is not necessarily able to spell it correctly. If we recognise that reading is a process of decoding which is supported by many different cues – graphophonics, meaning and structural cues – and that spelling is an encoding process in which the child has to construct words from her/his own resources, it is possible to see that accurate spelling requires much more specific knowledge of language than does reading.

Our research and that of others shows that reading and spelling are different but reciprocal processes which inform each other. Frith's developmental model, discussed earlier (Frith, 1985), highlights this. She suggests that children progress through logographic (whole word), alphabetic (analytical) and orthographic stages as both readers and spellers, but that reading and spelling development tend to proceed out of step and that at each phase learning in one area leads and informs development in the other.

Frith's argument was confirmed by the spelling and reading development of the case study children. While knowledge involved in reading and spelling is, clearly, reciprocal, nonetheless the case study children – once they had gone beyond the early 'analytic' stage of making links between sounds and letters – were invariably able to read many more words accurately, earlier, than they could spell them, in some cases very much earlier. In terms of Frith's model, while their writing continued at an 'alphabetic/analytic' stage, their reading had moved on and was much more 'orthographic' in character, with children reading in chunks and using a growing knowledge of common letter strings, as well as drawing on other cueing systems.

Samantha and Morgan both read with some fluency and accuracy by the time they were in Year 1, but their spelling, while developing competently in different ways, was far from being standard.

Daniel, an older child who experienced considerable difficulties with both reading and spelling, did not really begin to progress as a speller until his reading had reached a more independent level. This kind of information from the case studies shows, as Frith suggests, that for many children at the orthographic stage reading development leads the way and provides children with essential opportunities for observing and making inferences about the spelling system.

From our case studies it is therefore possible to hypothesise that:

- *in reading*, children's ability to segment words at the level of the individual phoneme (or sound) is likely to develop later than their knowledge of words as wholes (Frith, 1985; Moustafa, 1997);
- *in spelling*, however, a different process occurs. For most children their first recourse in attempting to spell words is through identifying individual and predominant phonemes, followed by more complete representations.

Therefore, phonemic awareness plays a more significant role at the early stages of spelling than in the early stages of reading (Bradley and Huxford, 1994). Furthermore, children's early spelling experiences actually help them to become more analytical about the phonemic aspects of reading words. The role of phonics in reading and spelling could therefore be expressed as follows:

Phonological and phonemic knowledge seem to play an important role in children's early spelling development. However, as different children learn in different ways and favour different strategies, it is important to emphasise many routes, rather than a single path, into spelling. For these reasons, it is important to consider a number of other areas of children's developing spelling knowledge.

2 Letter name and alphabetic knowledge

For most children, one of the first experiences of letter names and symbols is through their introduction to the alphabet – through an interest in their own names, alphabet songs and books. In learning the alphabet or how to spell their name, children are generally introduced (usually by their parents) to the names of letters, rather than their 'sounds'. Children's use of letter names as an early spelling strategy was seen frequently in the case studies in the first two years of school. When Dominic (Year 1) wrote:

| Gos | for | *goes* |
| fas | for | *face* |

and Elaine (Year 1) wrote

| Mi | for | *my* |

they clearly assumed that the vowels they used would sound like their letter names. Some case study children also drew on letter names at quite late stages in their spelling. This was particularly true in the case of long vowels in the middle of words; children seemed to use letter names either to replace a vowel digraph or to make a long vowel sound which should have been marked by a final 'e', e.g. *hide, gate*. Samantha (Year 1) wrote:

| Red | for | *read* |

Daniel (Year 4) wrote:

| Mad | for | *made* |

Letter names clearly play an important part in children's spelling in the earliest stages, but their use is a strategy which is normally abandoned relatively quickly

3 A repertoire of known words

Before children are able to hypothesise or generalise about the spelling system, they are involved in building up a repertoire of known words – words they have met often, or words which interest them. Samantha, aged 5 years and 4 months, wrote the following words she said she knew how to spell:

dog	cow
cat	go
the	on
to	it
is	I

Samantha particularly enjoyed making books from a young age; some of these books were made at school and some at home. In conversation with her in Years 1 and 2 it became clear that she wrote these texts for two very different reasons. First and foremost she took great pleasure in creating stories of her own, but she also spent a great deal of her leisure time copying – verbatim – whole texts, from favourite story books. Why?

Researcher:	This book you've made called *Who Ate the Bananas*? Was the idea of the title yours?
Samantha:	No. I copied it. I got it from a Sunshine book.
Researcher:	So, did you copy this [the text] from a Sunshine book?
Samantha:	Yes.
Researcher:	Right. Lots of children I know love copying stories out of books. Can you tell me why you like doing it?
Samantha:	Well, because when I was a bit younger about 6 or 5 I couldn't write very well and I couldn't spell properly. So I decided to start getting books and copying them and that way I could read them …
Researcher:	But it's really quite hard work to copy out the whole story isn't it?
Samantha:	Yes.

Researcher:	So, do you think it helps you as a reader or writer to write out the whole story?
Samantha:	Yeh.
Researcher:	How would it help writers, Samantha?
Samantha:	Well, I look at the words when I write the story and that helps me remember how to spell them.

In effect, Samantha had worked out a self-study programme for herself which, however arduous, gave her pleasure and a sense of achievment.

For older children, particularly those experiencing difficulties, building a repertoire of known words played a positive role, especially if the words were used as a basis for spelling new words through analogy Daniel, who had had considerable spelling difficulties during the project significantly pointed out by the end of the project that he could spell 'light' because he knew how to spell 'night'.

The role of memorisation

In the case of some older children we were struck by the role which memorisation played in supporting their knowledge (alongside other strategies). At the beginning of the project we were unsure about the efficacy of spelling tests but have been helped to modify our ideas. For some children, activities which focused on careful looking and committing to memory – whether it was words which had a common pattern or words which arose in a child's writing – were more beneficial than we had anticipated.

Spelling tests were sometimes helpful to children when they were based on:

- words with common letter patterns including prefixes and suffixes which supported the role of analogy making (clearly these were linked to children's development)
- words arising from children's own writing
- words children were continually encountering in well-known books and stories, topics or areas of subject knowledge
- techniques for learning spellings such as Look–Say–Cover–Write–Check

Anna said:

> The words we do are always similar in some way – endings like '-ely' or '-ier'. Spelling tests are only difficult when the words are all different and have nothing in common. Then you have to remember all the parts of every individual word.

But spelling tests which consisted of arbitrary lists of words tended to compound difficulties for inexperienced spellers. Such tests reinforced the tendency to look at words as disconnected individual units rather than helping children to categorise words through looking first at their similarities such as similar roots, letter patterns prefixes or suffixes.

4   Knowledge of visual patterns

At the earliest stages of writing, when children are scribbling, they take on some of the global elements of how writing looks in their home language (Harste *et al.*, 1984). So even at the very early stages there is some visual sense of the way that words in the language look, although at a very general level (Ferreiro and Teberosky, 1979). Later on, in attempting to spell a word, many young children write the initial letter and then use a configuration of letters to approximate the shape and length of the word in question. For instance, Samantha, in her labelling of the parts of the body in a diagram (see Fig. 4.1) writes *hmer* for *hair* and *hiem* for *heart* and later on she wrote *wererter* for *weather*. Here, the extraneous letters appear to be acting as 'placeholders'; they are used in an attempt to reproduce the overall 'look' or length of a word.

Even at the very early stages children seem to know that certain letter sequences never appear at the beginning of a word, e.g. *ck*, or that *q* is invariably followed by *u*. Margaret Peters points out that this arises more from experiences of print, rather than explicit teaching (Peters, 1993). In fact, she argues, children begin to notice patterns and features of print rather than the spellings of individual words.

This can be most clearly observed from children's early over-generalisations of particular orthographic features.

When Elaine wrote *mack* for *make* and Lucy wrote *tack* for *take* and *wock* for *woke* they were creating hypotheses. In these instances they were using letter names to represent vowel sounds and letter combinations which frequently appear together as the ends of words.

Margaret Peters stresses the importance of children's growing awareness of the 'serial probability' of letters in English spelling, i.e. which letters are likely to go together. Peters and other researchers have rightly stressed the importance of the transitional period in children's spelling development when they move from being mostly reliant on sound and are beginning to take on more and more of the orthographic features of the spelling system.

For instance, Eliot, a fluent speller, commented in Year 3:

> Spelling's quite hard sometimes. When you say it, you can't spell it the way it says. It's in another way.

> I still need help with spelling because I use hard, long words to do writing now and I try to say it. With words like 'mosquito' – you think it has a 'k' in it but it has a 'q'.

As children become more aware of the orthography of the English spelling system, their ability to map words and parts of words onto a range of possible alternative letter strings and patterns becomes increasingly refined. Their developing competence shows an ability to make choices which are increasingly complex and involve:

- Words which sound alike and are spelled alike: *dash, lash, cash*
- Words which sound alike and look different: *bear, bare, pair*
- Words which look alike and sound different: *done, gone, one*

Homophones: words with the same sound and different spellings

At the earlier stages of spelling, children drew on their existing knowledge of words they could already spell such as the use of *wood* for *would*. Among our case study children, spelling miscues based on homophones were particularly frequent in the case of older, less experienced spellers. It seemed that these inexperienced writers did not attend sufficiently to both the visual aspect and meaning of certain words as they made choices in their writing; instead they relied heavily on the primacy of sound in their spelling strategies (Table 4.1).

Where children were beginning to develop a greater linguistic awareness of word structures and meanings, this made a highly significant contribution to their spelling knowledge. This fact has clear

Table 4.1 Common confusions over words with the same sound and different spelling

Child's spelling	Intended word	Child	Year
there	they're	Samantha	Year 2
no	know	Samantha	Year 2
wood	would	Lucy	Year 3
wood	would	Florina	Year 4
their	there	David	Year 5
witch	which	David	Year 5
toad	towed	David	Year 5
their	there	Robert	Year 5
there	their	Kimberly	Year 5
their	there	Graham	Year 6
new	knew	Hannah	Year 6
there	their	Anna	Year 6
witch	which	Anna	Year 6
pore	pour	Anna	Year 6

Table 4.2 Developments in Morgan's spelling over a two-year period

Morgan's spelling	Standard spelling	Age	Developing Spelling Knowledge
saia bais	sausage bread	5yrs 10mths	initial sounds/phonemes plus placeholders
godn gadan	golden garden	6yrs 4mths	predominant phonemes, long and short vowel sound, syllabification
redeing	reading	6yrs 9mths	predominant phonemes, long vowels, suffix 'ing'
hospitall	hospital	7yrs 2mths	spelling a 3-syllable word, use of analogy for ending 'all'
boxs	boxes	7yrs 4mths	generalising about plurals
piking	picking	7yrs 5mths	short vowel with suffix 'ing'
famley	family	7yrs 5mths	based on her pronunciation, assuming a 2-syllable word
picked	picked	7yrs 9mths	Now uses *ck* correctly and *ed* suffix

implications for considering the kinds of teaching which will support children's achievement in spelling. It is important to draw children's attention to some structural features of words from early on, but especially important when analysis of children's spellings shows that they are beginning to be more aware of these features.

5   Spelling knowledge

The period of development of spelling knowledge lasts for a long time – most children will have become fluent readers long before a similar competency is acquired in spelling. It is a key time in children's development during which they need most support from teachers. Competent spellers like Eliot seemed to know early on what 'looked right' but teachers need to find ways of helping all children to make informed choices about their spelling. In other words, children need support in developing what Margaret Peters calls *spelling knowledge* – rather than an over-emphasis on the phonological aspects of spelling development.

The examples above (Table 4.2) taken from Morgan's spelling show the many different kinds of knowledge that were revealed in her development. As children become more competent as speakers, writers and thinkers, the demands on them as writers become greater. The written genres they engage with require increasingly complex language structures, styles, vocabulary and syntactical features. These genres call upon a wider range of linguistic competences, including nuances of meaning; these widening competences are also reflected in how children make choices about spellings. In this section, therefore, we examine how children's developing syntactic and semantic knowledge informs their spelling knowledge.

The examples of children's spelling in the sections that follow are drawn from right across our case studies, and show how certain patterns of hypothesising and rule generation were common to many children as their spelling knowledge expanded. But it also became clear that some children took on certain linguistic features earlier than others. The children's misspellings illustrated were not simply mistakes but miscues, indications of their thinking and hypothesising. To illustrate this, in selecting the examples we have focused on certain features in children's development and made some tentative observations which have implications for teaching.

6   Syntactic elements in spelling

Children's implicit and explicit grammatical understanding – their understanding of word structures and functions – became an important part of their growing spelling knowledge as they wrote longer and more complex texts. In order to take on the structural aspects of spelling, children began to attend less to the sounds of words and more to the ways in which words were structured. They perceived that certain grammatical word endings were marked by particular spellings. Focusing on the structural aspects of spelling enabled us to track children's growing understanding of these factors. Here, we have chosen to focus on ways in which children took on *-ed*, *-ing*, consonant doubling and plurals. As Table 4.3 shows , the case study children made progress in spelling at very different rates. A child in Reception and a child in Year 3 were making similar hypotheses. Lydia established the use of *-ed* by the end of Year 1 whereas Robert, identified as having some difficulties with spelling was still using a mainly phonetic approach to *-ed* in Year 4.

The use of the suffix *-ing* (Tables 4.4, 4.5) seemed to present few difficulties to the case study children. There were many instances of the standard use of *-ing* in Reception and Years 1 and 2, due presumably to the ease with which the sound of *-ing* transparently maps on to the letter string. What gave children more difficulty however, were the modifications that had to be made to verb endings when attaching *-ing*, or the doubling of consonants, where this was required. The following examples show that several children across the primary range were not sure about what should happen when *-ing* or *-ed* were attached to (mainly one syllable) verbs ending in a consonant. Lucy, who had established *-ed* in Year 2, did not begin to double consonants consistently until Year 4.

Table 4.3 Use of –ed: moving from sound to structure

Child's spelling	Standard spelling	Child	Year
opend	opened	Laura	Reception
oapd	opened	Natalie	Year 2
jumt	jumped	Florina	Year 2
marid	married	Kyle	Year 3
lookt	looked		
workt	worked		
plad	played		
stad	stayed		
agred	agreed	Sarah Year 3	
marryed	married	Lucy	Year 3
mayed	made	Sarah	Year 3
tride	tried	Robert	Year 4

Table 4.4 Examples of early hypotheses about the use of –ing

Child's spelling	Standard spelling	Child	Year
hoppg	hopping	Samantha	Reception
litg	letting	Samantha	Reception
tring	trying	Samantha	Year 1
phoneing	phoning	Samantha	Year 1
wakeing	waking	Lucy	Year 3

Table 4.5 Consonant doubling and the use of –ing and –ed

Child's spelling	Standard spelling	Child	Year
puting	putting	Julian	Year 2
droped	dropped	Samantha	Year 3
poped	popped	Lucy	Year 3
droped	dropped	Lucy	Year 3
stoping	stopping	Florina	Year 4
geting	getting	Christopher	Year 4

Use of plural forms

There seemed to be detectable patterns in the development of plural forms and their use by the case study children.

Very early on children found it relatively easy to simply add *-s* as in *eggs* (Dominic, Reception), and *cholips* (*tulips*) (Sarah, Year 2). At the same time, what was very striking among our case studies was the widespread use of the apostrophe 's' as opposed to a simple plural form. Perhaps children hypothesised initially that the apostrophe is a visual device to be applied to all words ending in s, before they came to understand its grammatical role. Eliot, an experienced speller, frequently used the apostrophe in this way even at the beginning of Year 3, but by the end of the year this error had virtually disappeared from his writing.

7 Semantic elements in spelling

Suffixes and prefixes

Children's growing understanding of word roots, word structures and their meanings, including prefixes and suffixes, played an increasing role in their ability to make the right choices when spelling a word. In observing these aspects of children's spelling, we were struck by the fact that they were writing texts which made increasing demands on their spelling, because of the complexity of the vocabulary they used. We have focused here on suffixes and prefixes (Table 4.6).

In the case studies, there were many more examples of words employing suffixes than prefixes. In fact, we found relatively few examples of use of prefixes at all before Year 4, and after that they were relatively rare. On one level this may have reflected children's own language use and the knowledge acquired from the kinds of reading and writing they have encountered. On another level it may have reflected insufficient attention to word study and explicit teaching in this area. Word study and grammar has been given greater focus through the National Literacy Strategy; as a result it may be expected that this aspect of children's language has developed.

8 Making analogies and deducing rules

As children became more experienced as readers and spellers, they made more use of analogies in order to read and spell unfamiliar words. Through making analogies they came to see that the written language system is not arbitrary. The emphasis in analogy theory has generally been on the phonological aspects of reading and spelling, but analogy making seemed to be much broader than that and was used in many different ways as children read and spelled unfamiliar words.

Analogy is important at many different points in children's spelling development: it is a basic learning strategy which enables children to detect patterns and generalise from known examples. In reading, and probably in spelling, it seems likely from recent work by Goswami that phonological awareness is the

Table 4.6 Examples of children's hypotheses about suffixes

Child's spelling	Standard spelling	Child	Year
cufterbul	comfortable	Samantha	Year 2
cefel	careful	Kyle	Year 3
poisones	poisonous	Sarah	Year 3
butiful	beautiful		
saflie	safely	Christopher	Year 4
saintest	scientist	Robert	Year 4
millean	million	David	Year 5
center	centre		
continant	continent	Christopher	Year 5
luckely	luckily		

factor underpinning children's ability to use analogy. As children's understanding grows they use their developing knowledge to predict patterns – whether these are phonetic, visual or linguistic – and to deduce rules. Gradually, hypothesising and making analogies form the basis for understanding the 'rules' of the system. This process can be summarised as follows:

Implicit knowledge ⟶	**Explicit knowledge**
Making analogies	
Hypothesising	Deducing rules
Forming generalisations	

This process – of making implicit knowledge explicit – signifies an important role for the teacher as well as opportunities for children to hypothesise through their own writing and in word study activities.

Gentry (1987) points out that there are relatively very few rules in English spelling that work without exception. What is more important is that children develop a sense of probability in selecting a particular spelling pattern – and using different kinds of knowledge to come to a decision about the most appropriate choices.

Good spellers seem to be able to make connections between remembered spelling patterns. They organise and categorise these patterns in their memory at the same time leaving space for exceptions and words that break the 'rules.' It is clear that analogy-making is a strategy common to many different areas of learning and that it is available from an early age. But it is also important that this key learning strategy is exploited by teachers and explicitly introduced to children.

9   Integrating different kinds of knowledge

As with any new learning, the strategies children adopted in their early spelling were influenced by their experiences of literacy and preferred styles of learning. Our case studies of young children beginning school show that they tended to show a significant preference for a particular strategy – phonetic, visual, or a reliance on copying. But what was important in terms of progress and development was that children should be able, over time, to integrate different kinds of strategies and draw on different kinds of knowledge, whatever their particular starting point.

Shareen (aged 7 years 8 months), whose particular learning strategy (discussed in Chapter 1) was based on accuracy at all costs (i.e. a desire to rely solely on copying correct forms), began to become more exploratory as she began to write more and engage with the spelling system. (There are many other examples of this amongst the case studies.)

> He felt a bit more hugrey and stoped to eat a shop ... he got to the market and saw a warter fonten.

> *(He felt a bit more hungry and stopped to eat a shop ... he got to the market and saw a water fountain.)*

As Shareen began to generate a range of spellings independently she demonstrated through generalisations and even overgeneralisations (*fellt*) that she had a range of different kinds of spelling knowledge on which to call. She continued to draw on known words which were firmly established in her memory e.g. *eat* and *shop*, while drawing on phonological strategies in *fonten* (*fountain*) and structural knowledge for the *-ed* in *stoped*. All spellers, whatever their starting point, needed to integrate different kinds of spelling knowledge and different strategies for spelling, widening their initial dependence on one or two strategies, and learning to use these strategies flexibly and appropriately

Those learners who were more likely to rely on what they heard needed to take into account the visual aspects of the English spelling system and to attend more consciously to the look of words. Those who relied more on visual memory needed to relate that knowledge to the sound system of English. The notion of stages is, therefore, a slightly misleading one because what denotes a particular 'stage' may simply be the dominance of one strategy over another – rather than the use of a single strategy in an exclusive sense.

However, analysis of children's early self-initiated spelling also shows that although one particular spelling strategy – such as use of phonetic spelling – may dominate, other strategies such as memory of known words will also be evident from early on.

> From the beginning children take advantage of what they know about the phonological forms of spoken words, the names of letters and the sequences of letters that make up printed words. If this is true, spelling is unlikely to progress through a series of qualitatively distinct stages in which different sources of knowledge are used. Development should be more continuous reflecting gradual improvements in children's phonological and orthographic knowledge.
>
> (Treiman, 1994)

In addition, development occurs within and between the different kinds of knowledge. As children gain more experience their attempts at phonetic spelling will become more plausible. Similarly, their ability to draw on orthographic knowledge (of letter patterns) or linguistic knowledge (of word structures and meanings), will be extended as their experience grows, and as they learn more about written language through engaging with it as readers and writers and through direct teaching.

Summary

Because of the nature of the English spelling system and the variety of learning styles and levels of experience in any classroom, it is important that children are helped from the beginning to develop a fuller understanding of how English spelling works and to use a range of strategies. Based on our observations, the evidence presented in this chapter and the following case studies, it is clear that the following areas of spelling knowledge are essential in the teaching and learning of spelling. Progress in spelling involves:

Extensive experience of written language

This experience will be gained through engaging with a wide variety of texts of all kinds (both read and written). Explicit teacher demonstrations, drawing attention to features of texts, are likely to be especially helpful in developing children's awareness of the features of written language.

Phonological awareness

Through development of phonological awareness (syllabification, onset and rime, phonemic awareness), children learn to attend more closely to increasingly detailed aspects of sound–letter relationships and to detect patterns of sound which are associated with patterns of letters.

Letter names and alphabetic knowledge

Knowing and using the names, sounds and forms of letters is an essential part of learning to spell.

Known words

Children learning to spell should be acquiring a growing lexicon of familiar words which are spelled correctly and which form the basis for analogy making.

Visual awareness

Spellers need to know that spelling is as much to do with how words look as how they sound. Visual awareness includes a growing sense of the likely patterns of letters that occur in English and the habit of looking at words within words and noting how words are made up.

Awareness of common letter strings and word patterns

Children need to become familiar with common letter patterns (e.g. *-at, -ad, -ee, -ing, -one, -ough*) including patterns in words that sound alike and look alike, and patterns in words which look alike but don't sound alike.

Knowledge of word structures and meanings

An increasing linguistic knowledge of word structures and meanings is part of children's development as spellers, and is evident in attention to

- prefixes (e.g. interval, international)
- tenses (e.g. *-s, -ing, -ed*, as in *laughs, laughing, laughed*)
- words made up of smaller words (e.g. *football, birthday*)
- word roots (e.g. *happy, unhappy, happiness; sign, signature* and *resignation*)
- word origins (e.g. *photograph, photosynthesis*)

Growing independence

Learning how to become independent spellers, knowing how and where to get help, how to use dictionaries, how to proof read and check their own and others' work, are all important in the learning of spelling. In addition to habits of self-monitoring, children need to have effective ways of consciously learning new spellings.

Making analogies and deducing rules

Making analogies, hypothesising and forming generalisations are the fundamental processes that help children to make sense of the spelling system. Much of children's learning at the early stages will be implicit; later on as their spelling knowledge grows children can become more reflective, able to make more explicit generalisations and deduce rules.

Teaching strategies to develop all these competences at both Key Stage 1 and Key Stage 2 were collected and classified in the course of the project and are included in the later chapter on this topic (Chapter 6, 'The effective teaching of spelling'.

The next chapter will consider in more detail the individual case studies of children as spellers, over a three-year period, which provided the main data for the project.

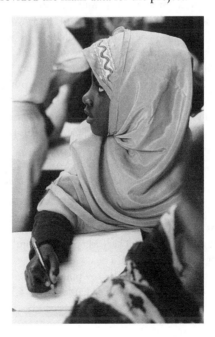

Chapter 5

The case studies

This chapter introduces case studies of individual children of different ages and with different learning styles who were followed over the three-year period of the project. In the previous chapter the case study material was drawn on in a general way, in order to identify and illustrate significant factors in spelling development. In this chapter, however, the aim is to provide more detailed and reflective accounts of six children's individual development over time. The studies provide insights into children's development within the classroom context and discuss teaching as well as learning.

Initially, 31 children, over half of whom were developing competently as spellers, were selected as case studies. They were from a variety of socio-economic, cultural and linguistic backgrounds; girls and boys were equally represented. At the end of the first year, it was decided to focus more closely on a core group of twelve children, while continuing to collect data from the wider group. All the case studies presented here are from the core group.

Over the three years we visited the schools twice per term to talk with the children and collect samples of their writing. There were discussions with teachers at least once per term. Conferences with children included discussion of individual pieces of writing as well as their approaches to spelling and their views of their own progress. Clearly, younger children found it more difficult to articulate their strategies and views about spelling than did older children. As we began to know the children better, it was possible to be more analytical with them about their writing and to discuss issues about their development in more detail with their teachers.

Spelling Assessment Framework

A significant factor in our understanding of children's spelling progress came through the development of an Assessment Framework for analysing children's strategies as spellers. This framework grew out of the work of Margaret Peters and Brigid Smith (1993), who developed a diagnostic grid to analyse children's miscues as spellers. Their work signalled the importance of studying what children are actually doing as they write and spell words. The Peters and Smith diagnostic grid uses four columns moving from 'Random', through 'Invented', to 'Plausible', which has two sub-categories: 'Readable' and 'Unreadable'. These categories clearly reflect their purpose: the diagnosis of spelling difficulties in working with older children. For the purposes of this project, however, which had as one of its main aims the analysis of younger children's spelling development, there were problems in using these particular headings as they did not provide a clear enough picture of children's developing competences.

The headings of the CLPE Spelling Assessment Framework (see Fig. 5.1) enabled analysis of the strategies a child was using and provided the necessary evidence for mapping children's development from year to year.

These categories helped analysis of the case study children's writing as the project proceeded through analysis of all the strategies that children were using as spellers. The framework showed clear patterns of development from right to left across the grid. The 'early phonetic' and 'early visual' categories allowed children's different early strategies to be recorded. The use of the categories 'visual strategies' and 'structural and semantic strategies' allowed a focus on the key point when children's orthographic (spelling) knowledge was developing. The framework is discussed at length in Chapter 7.

PART 1

Three children who made good progress as spellers

Three children have been chosen from the core group to illustrate different patterns of spelling development: two young children who were observed from Reception to Year 2 and an older child who was observed from Year 3 to Year 5.

In each case study there is a description of the child's progress over each year of the project, illustrated by writing examples, commentary and analyses using the CLPE Spelling Assessment Framework. At the end of each case study key factors are identified in teaching and learning.

The three children described here made good progress as spellers – however, there were distinct patterns to their learning:

Dominic, a phonetic speller: Reception – Year 2
Dominic took a considered approach to reading and writing and spelling. He spoke English as a main language, but also spoke French.

Samantha, a visual speller: Reception – Year 2
Samantha was a young fluent reader and writer. The interplay between her development as a reader and writer was significant. In both she was a risk-taker, tending to favour a visual approach.

Eliot, an early competent speller: (Years 3–5)
Eliot was a fluent reader, writer and speller from an early age. The influence of his teacher on his writing proved highly significant in his later progress.

Words spelled in standard form	Structural and semantic Visual strategies	Phonetic	Early phonetic Early visual	Pre-linguistic
All correctly spelled words	Errors associated with the structure and meaning of words Errors associated with the visual aspect of spelling	Attempts to represent most surface sounds	Early attempts to represent major sounds in words Early attempts to represent the look of words	Words which show little understanding of the writing system

Figure 5.1 Headings of the CLPE Spelling Assessment Framework

Dominic: a phonetic speller
Reception – Year 2
Languages: English/French

Reception

On first coming to school Dominic was reluctant to write. Drawing was his preferred medium. However, on one occasion in October he used a succession of 'r's' to represent the growling of Big Barney (a TV character) – this was an encouraging sign (see Example 1). His drawings were bold, detailed and of a high standard; they usually dominated the page. During this period his teacher or classroom assistant supported his writing by scribing for him. This teaching strategy was crucial: it demonstrated to Dominic how writers behave and gave him the confidence to have a go. By November he was beginning to participate independently in writing activities, though only venturing a few words (e.g. 'BIFF h D A I', which read 'Biff had a dream'). He still lacked confidence at this stage and needed much help and encouragement to discover how to use what he already knew about English spelling. In February, March and April drawing continued to be more important to him than writing, although his texts were now ten to fifteen words long.

On 25 April he wrote a clearly composed piece about noise and trying to sleep (see Example 2). He was beginning to know and use one or two key words e.g. *I, me, this,* and was able to pick out and record some of the major sounds in words, often using letter names to represent long vowel sounds (e.g. *woc* for *woke*). His confidence grew over the summer months, although he still never chose to write at length. In nine months he had made steady progress. He had moved from not writing at all (at school) to writing short texts of 10 to 15 words. He used his growing knowledge of phonetic possibilities together with a small repertoire of known words. However, it was clear that drawing continued to be more significant to him than writing.

Example 1 Dominic, Reception, Term 1, 5yrs 1mth   *Example 2* Dominic, Reception, Term 3, 5yrs 7mths

Year 1

On 11 September Dominic wrote about a holiday event; the text was fifteen words long and significantly he chose not to illustrate it. It was all about going to a dance and the last few words were 'I likt et I wotteb to stay' (I liked it I wanted to stay). This was the first time, according to all available evidence, that he had used writing to record a personal reflection. Later that month, he wrote a piece of information writing on school in Victorian times. Writing predominated on the page and came first. Dominic was still at the early stages of spelling but was now more willing to take risks using phonetic strategies. He was inclined to spell words as he pronounced them, for instance *woth* for was, *hith* for *his* and *taybool* for *table*. There was a pronounced focus in the classroom on explicit phonics teaching which, at this stage, Dominic found very helpful in his writing.

In the second half of the year it was obvious that Dominic had found his voice as a writer. He wrote poems, retold stories and wrote about his best friend. The following text was written in collaboration with another child but showed Dominic's usual sensitivity and thoughtfulness: 'This is my best friend. He is varry kind I really like him. He is just rit'. In pieces of unsupported writing Dominic continued to favour a phonetic approach to spelling; he had a relatively small repertoire of known words and chose to draw upon phonetic strategies rather than visual ones. This was particularly evident in a piece of information writing on ladybirds written in June which was an extended text of some 115 words (see Example 3 and Spelling Assessment 1). He was fired with enthusiasm and commitment in this piece of writing because of the topic. This was an important year in Dominic's progress as a writer and speller.

Ladybirds
The ladybird's lays eggs the ladybird's lay 1500 egg's. and wane the egg's hahc thea cold grub's. and the ladybird's lay egg's on roseboshis ... the ship went to O-maryca and it (the ladybirds) lad moe and theos lay more thean thea was lods and then the Australian's (copied) faod awt that O-marycan's did not hav muh chrubal. Becos theay hade ladybird's ....

Ladybirds
The ladybird's lays eggs the ladybird's lay 1500 eggs. And when the eggs hatch they are called grubs. and the ladybirds lay eggs on rosebusbes... the ship went to America and it (the ladybird) laid more and those lay more then there was loads and then the Australians found out that Americans did not have much trouble. Because they had ladybird's....

CLPE Spelling Assessment Framework

Name **Dominic**   Age 6yrs 9mths   Year group 1   Date/Term 17 June, Summer term

Languages **English/French**   Kind of writing **Information writing/narrative**

Words spelled in standard form	Structure and Meaning Visual patterns	Phonetic	Early		Pre-linguistic: little understanding of the spelling system
			Phonetic	Visual	
The (4) lays eggs lay (2) and cold and on... Substantial no of words – approx 100 written in standard form	ladybird's (ladybirds) x 15 lay's (lays) egg's (eggs) x3 grub's (grubs) to (two) abaot (about) want (went) x 2 moe (more) x2 yeas (years)	wane (when) boshis (bushes) O-maryca (America) x 2 lods (loads) awt (out) hav (have) x2 chrubal (trouble) becos (because) Amarycan's (Americans) sant (sent) cod (could) thean (then) thea (there) theat (that)	thea (they are) faod (found) hade ? (had)	hahc (hatch)	

What does the analysis show about the child's progress in spelling (eg patterns of development)? Note any areas that require particular teaching

Is developing substantial vocabulary of words he knows how to spell – is now writing at much greater length.

Dominic's use of letter string 'the' to begin a number of related words difficult to categorise as he is probably combining phonetic and visual strategies - sounds out known word the and then adds ending (early analogy making) - to be discussed with him.

Encouraage D to use look-say-cover-write check more effectively - relies too heavily on how words sound - needs to be helped to consider how words look. Help him to draw on words he already knows how to spell.

Total no of words 115

No of standard spellings 65

% of standard spellings 57%

No of miscues 50

% of miscues 43%

Example 3 and Spelling Assessment 1 Dominic, Reception, Term 1, 5yrs 1mth

Year 2

By the beginning of Year 2 Dominic's second language had become more important to him. He spent the long summer holiday in Bordeaux and returned with a greater understanding of the language and the country. He had the confidence to speak in French and talk about his experiences.

Dominic was writing at length in English when he returned to school in September. He chose to write about some toys (109 words) (see Example 4). He had built up a substantial list of known words and was attending to the sounds in words although there was some typical confusion with vowel sounds (*gat* for *get* for instance).

Toys Gat Lost
One day at nit some children wat on holiday. their names are Jason and Sam. They had a toyech Ted and Tim. they want on the coch. theyfogot the toys. Sam said war are the toys ....
Tele mum. O dare said mum the Teddy Bear's hade a advenchae. they met a cat they Beceam frands. Cat did not have a name and they calledit cat.

Example 4 Dominic, Year 2, Term 1, 7yrs 0mths

But in January February and March Dominic seemed to opt out of writing, producing minimal texts which were often hurried, e.g. 'On Sunday I watched Jery Luis, he is very funy I cannot stop laughing'. It became difficult to assess his progress as a speller with such short and often formulaic pieces. By the Summer, and with much encouragement and cajoling from his teacher, he had become a more committed writer and had also acquired a good cursive handwriting style which in turn seemed to support his fluency in spelling words (see Example 5 and Spelling Assessment 2). Punctuation, in particular full stops, was used to mark meaning; he did not often remember to put capital letters at the beginning of sentences. His repertoire of known words had increased considerably; however, he still relied mainly on phonetic strategies to spell unfamiliar words. A new and significant development became evident in a text at the end of June where he was generalising about the suffix 'ed' and using it willy-nilly wherever a word ended with a 'd' sound, e.g. 'goaled' for 'gold'.

Summary

Dominic's development as a writer and speller (and reader) was slow but sure. Many of his texts showed how thoughtful and committed he could be as a writer and speller.

It took him the best part of his first year in school firstly to want to write and secondly to take the

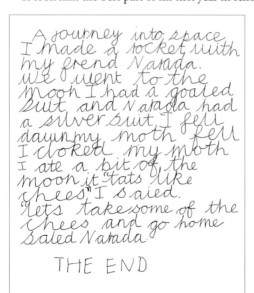

Example 5

necessary risks to become an independent writer. Drawing was his strength. He relied on his teachers to give him words and often his texts were limited to just a few words. This trend to write minimal texts persisted into Year 1 although writing at this stage was becoming more important to him and he felt he had something to say Occasionally he wrote at length and then it was possible to assess his spelling more accurately as in Example 4. He made a slow start in Year 2, only writing when pressure was applied. Later, as he became more involved with schoolwork and as his confidence grew, he wrote at more length and with interest.

His chief spelling strategy throughout was based on his developing knowledge of the relationship between sounds and symbols, although by Year 2 he was making very good use of his vocabulary of known words. His reading strategies were similar to those he applied to spelling, in that he favoured using phonics skills to tackle new words. Dominic also had an extensive repertoire of known words, both in spelling and reading, but had not developed much awareness of common visual patterns or letter strings in spelling.

Key elements in supporting Dominic's spelling were:

- At the early stages the teacher and classroom assistant scribed for Dominic both to support and encourage him as an author and also to demonstrate how language is written down.
- Up to the end of Year 1, Dominic saw drawing as more important than writing – his narratives seemed to take place through his drawing. By the end of Year 1, opportunities to write personally and expressively had begun to help Dominic to realise what writing could do for him and he began to write the occasional piece of up to a hundred words, although this was still a rarity.
- In terms of his spelling development Dominic had become very reliant, particularly in Year 1, on the use of a spelling book. He would ask for words to be written down and then copy them in his writing. During the course of that year, school policy began to explicitly encourage children to try out spellings before referring to the teacher or spelling book. This helped Dominic to become more independent as a speller.
- The development of a good cursive handwriting style by Year 2 seemed to support his spelling fluency.

CLPE Spelling Assessment Framework

Name *Dominic* Age *7yrs 9mths* Year group *2* Date/Term *June, Summer term*

Languages *English/French* Kind of writing *Narrative*

Words spelled in standard form	Structure and Meaning Visual patterns	Phonetic	Early		Pre-linguistic: little understanding of the spelling system
			Phonetic	Visual	
I x 6 made a x 4 rocket with my x 3 Narada x3 we went to the x 3 moon had suit x 2 and x 2 had silver suit fell x 2 ate bit of x 2 moon it like lets some go home	*goaled (gold)* *saied (said) x 2*	*frend (friend)* *dawn (down) x 2* *chees (cheese)* *tak (take)* *moth (mouth)* *cloked (closed?)*	*tats (tastes)*		

What does the analysis show about the child's progress in spelling (eg patterns of development)? Note any areas that require particular teaching

Vocabulary of words spelled in standard form has increased in number and complexity..

Despite this, still relies mainly on phonetic strategies with new words –suggest that D has time to look at some of his own texts with real intent – particular words highlighted for attention. Perhaps use short dictation to monitor progress.

Joined up handwriting now well established.

Total no of words *57*

No of standard spellings *46*

% of standard spellings *81%*

No of miscues *11*

% of miscues *19%*

Spelling Assessment 2

Samantha: a visual speller

Reception–Year 2
Languages: English

Reception

Samantha was 5 years old at the beginning of the Autumn Term of her Reception year which followed a fruitful start in the school's excellent nursery class. She was an enthusiastic writer from the beginning. In her first two months of school she communicated through writing using strings of letters, mostly upper case and usually written across the top of the page (see Example 1). Accompanying pictures commanded the best part of the page and formed an important part of what she wanted to say.

In November there was a shift away from writing strings of letters and the beginnings of an understanding of the permanent nature of spellings. She wrote words such as 'I' and 'the' in standard form on a consistent basis. By January words were deliberately spaced and she ventured to write twelve words she already knew – all spelt in standard form. In April she wrote, in role, a letter to Jack (in the Beanstalk) from the Giant and it was evident that she had amassed a number of known words. In unfamiliar words, in all cases she used the appropriate initial letter for each word she wrote (e.g. *s* in *sory* [sorry]; *p* in *pete* [party] ; *f* in *fies* [friend]). Samantha was probably drawing primarily on her memory of the visual features of particular words e.g. the *y* in *sory* and *ie* in *friend* (see Example 2).

Although by the end of the first year Samantha was using some phonetic strategies – initial letters – she was inclined to favour a visual approach in spelling. Her progress had undoubtedly been influenced by her wide and varied experience both as a writer and reader (e.g. stories, letters, lists, labelled diagrams, and story maps). The teacher's role in Samantha's rapid progress had been crucial: she had provided a learning environment where writing was considered both pleasurable and worthwhile and given a high profile. She modelled the writing process for the children, drawing on both personal experiences and on stories and texts they knew, using shared writing as the main medium. At the same time she encouraged all the children to have a go at writing and spelling for themselves and to draw on a wide range of available resources.

Example 1 Samantha, Reception, Term 1, 5yrs 1mth

Example 2 Samantha, Reception, 5yrs 6mths

Year 1

Samantha still loved to write – not at length but often and in a variety of forms (e.g. making books, writing letters and lists, making maps and plans, reporting on outdoor activities). She spent much of her free time at home copying out favourite stories or books, verbatim, an activity which continued into Year 2. She found it difficult to explain why this afforded her so much pleasure, other than it gave her a sense of achievement. In October, as part of a classroom topic on holidays, Samantha wrote a postcard to one of her friends. 'I im hoperg a good taim iv got a litteil ten I im going to biag a sieevn' '(I am having a good time. I've got a little tan. I am going to bring a souvenir).

Samantha drew on a diverse range of strategies: she used visual memory to write *I im* for 'I'm' and *litteil* for 'little'; a phonetic approach to write *taim* for 'time' and a somewhat more random approach – apart from the correct initial letter – for words such as *hoperg* for 'having' and *sieevn* for 'souvenir'.

Early on in Year 1 it was evident that Samantha, who was writing enthusiastically and sometimes at length, was building up a large repertoire of known words. At the same time, there was little evidence of her using this knowledge to predict the spellings of unfamiliar words. By the Summer term, and with direct teaching support, Samantha learned to make some links between how words sound and how words look (see Example 3).

One morning as the sun came up God's sister came along with a red dress on and the sun lit through her dress. The sky looked red because of the dress. Every day a boy drives a wagon across the sky and meet all different weather he saw rain and the sun and lightning and thunder he stopped to let it rain and to two men were flying and they got killed and went to stars.

CLPE Spelling Assessment Framework

Name *Samantha* Age *6yrs 4mths* Year group *1* Date/Term *Summer Term*

Languages *English* Kind of writing *Narrative*

Words spelled in standard form		Structure and Meaning Visual patterns	Phonetic	Early		Pre-linguistic: little understanding of the spelling system
				Phonetic	Visual	
One	as	drive's (drives)	becose (because)	mint (meet)	wererter (weather)	
the x 6	sun	stop (stopped)	thiro (through)	strs (stars)		
came x2	up	moning (morning)	wagan (wagon)			
God's	with	sester (sister)	thay (they)			
a x 3	red x 2	alog (along)	kild (killed)			
dress x2	on	liet (lit)				
and x 6	sun x 2	acrass (across)				
her	dress	linting (lightening)				
sky x 2	looked	leat (let)				
red x 2	of	fleing (flying)				
every	day	drifferent (different)				
boy	all					
he x 2	saw					
rain x 2	thunder					
to x 2	it					
two	men					
were	got					
went						

What does the analysis show about the child's progress in spelling (eg patterns of development)? Note any areas that require particular teaching

S is developing an extensive vocabulary of words she can spell in standard form. Is prepared to attempt spellings in a wide range of writing.

At present she is relying very much on how words look rather than how they sound - looks particularly at the beginnings and ends of words but doesn't look much at what lies in between. Encourage her to self-correct eg help her to see where letters are missing.

Total no of words 75

No of standard spellings 56

% of standard spellings 75%

No of miscues 19

% of miscues 25%

Example 3 and Spelling Assessment Samantha, Year 1, Term 3, 6yrs 4mths

Year 2

Samantha continued to write for pleasure, original pieces as well as copied stories. By this time her vocabulary of known words had increased considerably. Significantly, by October she had added phonetic strategies to her preferred visual approach and there was also a growing recognition of some of the grammatical features evident in spelling, for example using endings such as -ed or -ing. She also began to self-correct (for example, she had spelt 'haveing' retaining the 'e', and then subsequently crossed out the 'e').

She was now no longer seeing spelling as a multitude of unrelated words. Although she continued to take risks with unfamiliar words, her guesses were based on a more systematic understanding of the spelling system – from both a sound and a structural point of view. For example she spelled the words *looked*, *cooked* and *played* in standard form (see Example 5).

Encouraged by her teacher she was using full stops to mark meaning more intentionally and using contractions like 'I'm' and 'don't', although she overgeneralised about the use of the apostrophe. The quality of her writing varied enormously. When encouraged to write over time in a small group her writing was thoughtful and imaginative; at other times she didn't always set herself such high standards.

Her spelling at the end of Year 2 had progressed well; she usually managed to achieve at least 90% standard spelling across a wide range of genres (see Example 5). Although there were a number of slips of the pen she generally used an effective range of strategies with a distinct preference for a visual approach.

Summary

Samantha's individual learning style showed a preference for a visual approach for learning new words and this was particularly evident in the early years, not only in her spelling but also in her reading. Her greatest strength was her visual recall and due to this she developed a rapidly increasing repertoire of words that she could spell in standard form.

However, at the early stages, she often used visual approximations of words or parts of words. In order therefore for her to develop further as a speller, she needed to be encouraged to make links between words she knew and to generalise from this information. Samantha's teachers supported her

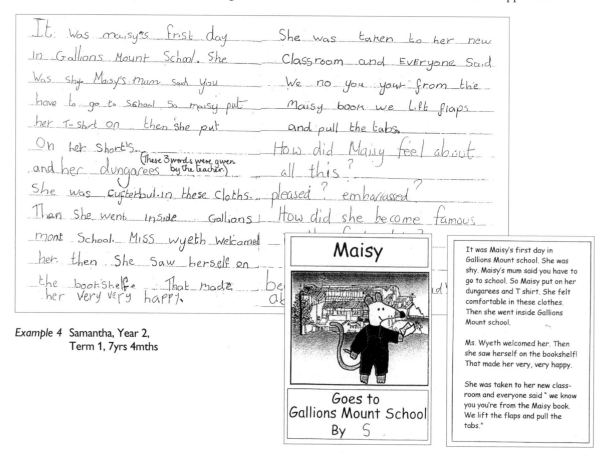

Example 4   Samantha, Year 2,
          Term 1, 7yrs 4mths

development by encouraging her to build on what she knew and to recognise the ways words are patterned – visually, phonetically and structurally. Her development was also fostered by her teacher's enthusiasm and high expectations in all literacy-related activities. By the middle of Year 2 Samantha was experienced enough to play a more active role in checking final drafts for common misspellings, and had become a confident and quite competent speller and writer, who initiated much of her own work. She was a competent reader. Throughout her development it was noticeable that as she became more analytical as a writer, this in turn fed into her development as a reader. Similarly, as she began to look more closely at words in her reading, this in turn informed her accuracy as a speller.

Key elements in supporting Samantha's development were:

- Her wide experience as a writer across a range of genres.
- Teacher demonstrations through purposeful shared writing, on a daily basis in the early period – with these models of writing frequently based on what had been read aloud.
- A balance between teacher-generated and modelled writing and opportunities for using writing in more personal ways and in play.
- The teachers' high expectations of children as readers and writers.
- A range of spelling resources, many classroom made, which were closely linked to children's interests and needs, made accessible and freely available (e.g. alphabets, lists of common words, words from core books currently being used as models for writing).
- Recognition by her teachers of Samantha's strength, which was her visual memory, together with a repertoire of known words. Teachers used this strength as a basis for further development, encouraging Samantha to begin to make analogies on the basis of what she knew.
- Thoughtful teacher intervention in her writing and spelling on a 1:1 basis.

The school trip
Class 9 was going on a school trip. It was very rainy. The teacher was not happy about the wether ... Sally was very bad because she kept mumbering ... We was going to the muic center Leon was always botharing us ... The teacher said I all want you to pik your favrite insterments. then you can draw the insterments ... Wait it's lunch time. I'm not hungey said Amy ... It was relly hard work. Hayligh played the clarernet. Hayligh was very nurvers ... But it was time to go it took two hours to get back ... did everyone have a good time yes.

CLPE Spelling Assessment   Framework

Name *Samantha*   Age *7yrs 9mths*   Year group 2   Date/Term *June, Summer Term*

Languages *English*   Kind of writing *Report*

Words spelled in standard form	Structure and Meaning Visual patterns	Phonetic	Early		Pre-linguistic: little understanding of the spelling system
			Phonetic	Visual	
A piece of 239 words - The school trip.	keept (kept) write (right) muic (music) center (centre) hungey (hungry) chiden (children) her slef (herself) hous (hours)	wether (weather) mumberling (mumbling) botharign (bothering) insterments (instruments) nely (nearly) favrite (favourite) instermants (instruments) instremants (instruments) relly (really) clarernet (clarinet)			

What does the analysis show about the child's progress in spelling (eg patterns of development)? Note any areas that require particular teaching

Growing number of words in standard form – now over 90%. Slightly increased proportion of miscues in phonetic column – show that Samantha is now bringing a full range of strategies to her determination to get the spelling right – as with 'instruments'. Continue to encourage her to be self-monitoring and help her to develop strategies for remembering difficult parts of words eg the strum in instruments.

Total no of words 239

No of standard spellings 220

% of standard spellings 92%

No of miscues 19

% of miscues 8%

Example 5 and Spelling Assessment Samantha, Year 2, Term 3, 7yrs 9mths

Eliot: an early competent speller

Year 3–Year 5
Language: English

Year 3

Eliot was 8 years old in September as he began Year 3. A piece written near the beginning of Year 3 was typical: entitled 'The spooky, spooky street' it was based on the picture book *A Dark, Dark Tale* and nearly 100 words in length: 'Once upon a time in a spooky spooky street in the street there's a spooky spooky road on the spooky spooky road there's a spooky spooky house…'. His early pieces of writing showed that his spelling was almost entirely standard and that he used very little punctuation, apart from occasional full stops. Misspellings were few and tended to be visual (e.g. *curtian*) or structural (e.g. the use of an apostrophe in plurals such as *dream's*). Very occasionally Eliot would resort to phonetic spellings, but even here he made pertinent analogies with words he knew (for example writing *curbird* for cupboard). His writing grew in length – by October he frequently wrote pieces of nearly 150 words and also began to develop his own voice as a writer.

His story *The famous boat race* written in the Spring term shows the clear effect of his reading on his writing, particularly in his use of language (see Example 1). In this piece of 135 words there were only 2 errors: one structural misspelling (*pasted* for *passed*) and one visual (*flouting* for *floating*). Over the year his use of punctuation also developed – including capitalisation, full stops, and speech marks. Because Eliot's spellings were almost entirely standard, the Spelling Analysis Framework was not used.

Later in the Spring term, two pieces of science writing showed that Eliot was beginning to handle technical vocabulary competently as both a writer and a speller (see Example 2). At this stage, his teacher tended to write out corrections of his occasional misspellings over the top of a word. Even though Eliot was a competent speller it would have probably been helpful to encourage him to work on particular aspects of his spelling in a spelling journal – such as work on plurals or to help him find ways of remembering the spelling of a word like *separate* (he wrote *seperate*).

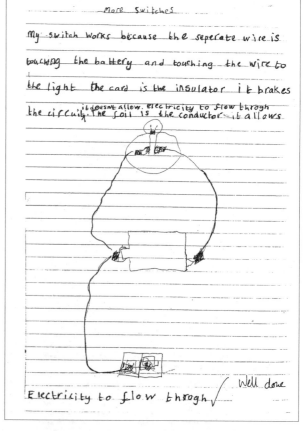

Example 1 Eliot, Year 3, Term 2, 8yrs 6mths

Example 2 Eliot, Year 3, Term 3, 8yrs 8mths

Year 4

During this year Eliot continued to spell most words in standard form. What became a more significant issue was the slowing down in his development as a writer and the effect of this on his growing understanding of language and spelling. For example in longer pieces of writing, Eliot tended to lose his thread towards the end and sometimes had problems with grammar – mainly because he was writing at greater length or in new forms. Greater emphasis on helping Eliot to develop and sustain his ideas through a piece of writing, or on talking through some of his more problematic sentences would have been particularly helpful. Eliot had not developed cursive handwriting 'Sometimes I join up, sometimes I don't because it looks messy We do handwriting practice in class.' At this point, the fact that he had not been helped to develop cursive handwriting was becoming a barrier to writing easily and legibly.

In March Eliot asked 'Did we look at my piece on Macbeth last time?' (see Example 3). The writing was a literal retelling of the story of Macbeth and was succinct, showing a sure grasp of some of the complexities of the plot. It was also notable that, despite these complexities, Eliot tended to stick to simpler words and would sometimes make grammatical errors, e.g. 'a army'. In his spelling, there were occasional errors (for example *thoght* for 'thought', twice in the same piece). His teacher corrected his work by writing corrections over his misspellings. It might have been more helpful to encourage him to work on the spelling pattern *-ought* or look at the need to double the consonant in the middle of *stabbed* (he wrote *stabed*).

At the end of Year 4 Eliot wrote a piece called *The Real Americans*, a story narrative with an adult flavour, which showed that Eliot had a growing sense of a particular genre and revealed the influence of TV on his writing (see Example 4). Once again, however, the piece indicated that spelling was not the main issue in terms of furthering Eliot's development as a writer. A greater focus was needed on helping him to structure his writing, widen his written vocabulary, and to address non-standard features such as the use of 'was' for 'were'. Much of this could have been achieved by helping him to pay closer attention to written texts of many kinds.

The Story of Macbeth.

One night Macbeth and Banquo were walking home from a war. At the top of the hill they saw three witches. The witches called Macbeth and told him and Banquo that Macbeth was going to be King and Banquo would be the father of the kings. Macbeth thought that was very strange and said to himself how he wouldn't be king because his only a Scottish general. When he got home he told his wife Lady Macbeth what had happened. Lady Macbeth told Macbeth to invite King Duncan and kill him. So he arranged for Duncan to come round. The night when Duncan came Lady Macbeth gave Macbeth the knife and Macbeth went in the living room and stabbed Duncan. Then Mabeth became King.

Example 3 Eliot, Year 4, Term 2, 9yrs 6mths

The real Americans

In 2026 2 brothers named Colin and Peter. Peter was tall, big built, black, brown eyes and was 30. Colin was short, skinny, black, blue eyes and was 28. They was both born in America. They was always getting in trouble by the police. One day came when they were both out on the booze. Then a gang of robbers came into the casino. Colin and Peter was half drunk playing on the fruit machines. The robbers was getting the money. Colin noticed the robbers and thought I won't go over until they have gone. Eventually they left with the money. Colin ran over to the phone box and dialed 911 and asked for the police. "Hello Police here" said a police officer. "Hello" said Colin "there's been a robbery here at the casino on sunset balvard". "Oh we'll send two police men down there", said the police officer. Colin put the phone down and waited for the police. Peter asked him What's the matter. "I'm just waiting for the police to come" said Colin. just that moment the police came. Colin told them everything. he told them they come every Thursday. So next Thursday came round and the robbers came. The police arrested the robbers. But Colin and Peter got arrested for setting them up.

Example 4 Eliot, Year 4, Term 3, 9yrs 6mths

Year 5

During the Autumn term of Year 5, Eliot was taught by a supply teacher. By the beginning of the Spring term, however, he had a new teacher who was helping the class to consider aspects of their writing. Eliot wrote a non-chronological piece entitled *Victorians at Home* and revealed that: 'We read through information pages and underlined all the adjectives which told you about homes in Victorian times, then you had to use these words in your own writing.' At the same time he was being encouraged to use cursive handwriting – and by March this was established.

Eliot was also being helped to sustain longer pieces of writing. In his story *The Magic Wardrobe* – for which he wrote a plan and sketched out characters – his new teacher made helpful interventions at both the planning stage and also at two points during the piece itself – encouraging him and making specific prompts. 'I didn't know how to end but Miss helped me' said Eliot.

By May, Eliot began to display once more aspects of a more literary style. In one piece he guessed at the word *devastated* and wrote *defistated*. His teacher congratulated him on a 'good word' and ticked the parts which were correct. In another piece about Demeter and Persephone his teacher congratulated him on 'some excellent expressions' (see Example 5). In an imaginative story *Underground Adventure*, Eliot showed how he was beginning to think much more carefully about choosing words. His teacher, responding as a reader, congratulated him on finding alternatives for *said* – he wrote 'suggested Tom' and 'replied Dave'.

During this time his teacher gave advice in her marking on Eliot's:

- use of tenses
- use of adverbs and adverbial phrases
- the development of plot
- developing a climax in the story
- effective use of language e.g. use of alternative words for words like *got*

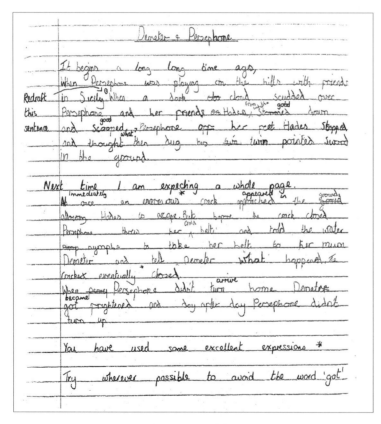

Example 5 Eliot, Year 5, Term 3, 10yrs 7mths

Summary

The case study of Eliot reveals the important connection between supporting children's progress in writing and furthering their spelling development. Despite the fact that Eliot spelled nearly 100% of words correctly, he still needed a great deal of support as a writer. During Year 4 his writing became less adventurous and he seemed to be limiting himself in his choice of vocabulary. The intervention of a teacher in the Spring and Summer terms of Year 5 played an important role in supporting his development in many areas. Although his spelling continued to be almost entirely correct, Eliot needed a great deal of further experience both in structuring and revising his writing, and in considering the needs of a reader.

Key elements in supporting Eliot's spelling development were:

- The role of the teacher in responding as a reader to his writing – commenting positively on his use of words, his use of information, and his story plots.
- In Year 5 his teacher supported him by helping him to structure his writing, to write at greater length and in new forms, to choose words to greater effect, to work on problems of syntax and Standard English, to consider audience and to find his own voice as a writer.
- The Year 5 teacher's interventions focused on particular aspects of his writing and spelling which he was beginning to develop.
- Children in the class were encouraged to discuss their writing beforehand.
- Texts of many kinds were used to provide models for writing.
- Writing was not planned as a series of 'one-offs'. By Year 5 Eliot was writing several pieces around a single topic (e.g. The Victorians) which included poems, accounts, stories; some pieces of writing were developed at length.

Conclusion to Part 1

These three case studies, showing children working in classrooms in different schools, confirm a number of significant factors about children's spelling progress and development.

- **Children take different routes into the spelling system**
  Children take different routes into the spelling system and develop as spellers in different ways. Dominic's route was primarily a phonetic one, while Samantha's was strongly influenced by her visual sense of written language.

- **Many different kinds of knowledge influence development in spelling**
  The development of Dominic, Samantha and Eliot confirmed that children needed to integrate different kinds of knowledge – phonetic, visual, structural and semantic – in order to develop effectively as spellers.

- **Writing plays a key role in promoting spelling development**
  In all three case studies, spelling development was supported by a wide range of writing experiences. As the children wrote widely and at increasing length, their spelling noticeably developed. In the case of all the children, the experience of writing in different genres widened their written vocabulary and therefore the range of words they were attempting to spell.

- **The teacher's role is crucial in children's progress as spellers**
  In all the case studies the role of the teacher was paramount in supporting development – not only in a general sense, in terms of planning a range of writing activities, but also, more particularly in terms of their intervention and support for children's spelling development at individual, group and class level.

Having considered the progress and development of three children who were developing competently as spellers, we now go on to consider the development of three children who were experiencing difficulties with spelling.

PART 2

Children in Key Stage 2 with spelling difficulties

The three case studies presented here address the spelling development of older children, one from each of the three schools. Two of the children had a discrepancy between their competence in reading and spelling; the third experienced more general difficulties in both areas.

Anna, an enthusiastic reader and writer
Years 4–6

Anna was an avid reader and writer who experienced many difficulties with spelling. She spoke both English and Italian. There was a clear mismatch between the fluency of her reading and her problematic spelling.

Jonathan, a competent reader and unenthusiastic writer
Years 4–6

Jonathan was reluctant to write and experienced some difficulties with spelling. His spelling developed alongside his growing confidence and experience as a writer, with the crucial support of his teachers.

Daniel, a child with profound difficulties with both reading and spelling
Years 3–5

Daniel was not able to make sense of the written code beyond initial letters at Year 3. However, he was increasingly willing to write freely, in spite of his difficulties. This case study contains an update on his progress in Year 6 because of our interest in his progress.

Anna: an enthusiastic reader and writer

Year 4–Year 6
Language: English/Italian

Year 4

Anna was selected as one of our case studies because she had been identified by her school as having difficulties with spelling, in spite of the fact that she read competently and with great pleasure. Although Anna was more competent in English than Italian she took an active interest in Italian, and spent every summer holiday in Italy. She understood the language and spoke it a little.

Anna was easy to talk with, and was able to articulate her achievements and specify her difficulties with spelling. Her chief spelling strategy with unfamiliar words was confined to thinking about syllabification and pronunciation prior to interpreting the sounds she identified into phonemes. She knew that this was not always entirely successful but found it difficult to draw on a wider range of strategies. In spite of her apparent difficulties she built up a substantial repertoire of known words and could compose with obvious ease and enjoyment. It was clear that Anna's wide experience as a reader influenced her composition more than her spelling (see Example 1 and Spelling Assessment 1). As the

Example 1 and Spelling Assessment 1 Anna, Year 4, Term 1,
8yrs 11mths

The One Eyed giant.

A very wery long time agow there lived a man called Odysseus. He lived with his wife Penelope. One day Odysseus was called to go to war with his fellow freinds. So he whent. 19 years later he had not returnd so thire were rumers that he, the bravenst of them all, had been killed by the enymes. But his wife did not whant to think that he, the bravist her hasbend had been killed Every morning yonhg men wold come and aske her to mary them but Penelope did not think that Odysseus was dead Sau...

CLPE Spelling Assessment Framework

Name *Anna*   Age *8yrs 11mths*   Year group *4*   Date/Term *November, Autumn*

Languages *English*   Kind of writing *Retelling a myth*

Words spelled in standard form	Structure and Meaning Visual patterns	Phonetic	Early		Pre-linguistic: little understanding of the spelling system
			Phonetic	Visual	
the x 4 One x 2 *Eyed giant* *a x 2 very x 2* *long time* *there lived x 2* *man Odysseus x 2* *he x 5 with x 2* *his x 3 wife x 2* *Penelope day* *was to x 2* *go x 2 fellow* *so x 2 years* *later had x 3* *not x 2 were* *that of* *them all* *been x 2 killed x 2* *by but* *did think her* *(plus a further 19 words)* *(Title and proper names were given)*	*wore (war)* *bravenst (bravest)* *agow* *cuold* *freinds* *whent* *whant*	*calld (called)* *reternd (returned)* *thire (there)* *romers (rumours)* *enyme's (enemies)* *hasbend* *(husband)* *mary (marry)* *aske (ask)* *bravist (bravest)*			*yonhg (young)*

What does the analysis show about the child's progress in spelling (eg patterns of development)?
Note any areas that require particular teaching
A is very enthusiastic about writing and has few inhibitions about spelling. Despite a wide vocabulary of known words, frequently turns to her preferred phonetic strategy with common words and less familiar ones.

Help A to identify a few misspellings in each piece to work on particularly common words, words with common patterns, and perhaps to look at inflectional elements of language such as call, called etc

Total no of words 99

No of standard spellings 82

% of standard spellings 83%

No of miscues 17

% of miscues 17%

year progressed Anna continued to write quite extensively and her teacher encouraged her to be more active in self-correcting her work and at times to edit with a partner. In the summer Anna talked openly about her confusion between spelling in Italian and English, 'In Italian you have to listen to the sounds of the words and I'm in a muddle with English 'cos that doesn't always work.'

First drafts of her writing in the latter half of the year continued to show how she concentrated on composition at the expense of spelling and punctuation. She quite often reversed letters in words (e.g. *holws* for *howls*, *lihgt* for *light*) and also ignored the need to mark meaning by using punctuation (see Example 2). It was noticeable that she occasionally used a dictionary to help her and made use of words that were on display in the classroom: all the children were taught how to use the available resources effectively. At this stage, she was not making good use of the Look–Say–Cover–Write–Check strategy.

Year 5

Anna wrote in a range of genres quite confidently (e.g. stories, descriptions, information writing, letters and playscripts). During this year Anna's teacher often helped her and the class as a whole to look with intent at word roots and structures. This contributed to Anna's progress through raising her awareness of the visual aspects of the spelling system and of common letter patterns (see Example 3). When she wrote *cry*, *cried*, *crying* and *hop*, *hopping*, *hopped* she had really understood the connections and from this was able to deduce helpful rules.

Throughout the year she continued to shape pieces of writing with thought and confidence and her handwriting changed into a joined script. She still made slip-of-the-pen errors, such as *with* for *white* but as soon as she began to take more responsibility for editing her work, using available resources and strategies, she became a more competent writer in the fullest sense.

This was a period of consolidation for Anna. She now had an extensive repertoire of known words and also commented that she was learning from her errors. While she was making progress and had a better understanding of the spelling system, she still experienced difficulty when spelling new words. She was willing to take risks – would always have a go – but from a range of possible spellings often found it difficult, or even impossible, to identify the standard spelling. This would involve reverting to phonetic strategies such as *ses* for *says* and *liyen* for *lion*.

Example 2 Anna, Year 4, Term 3, 9yrs 4mths

Example 3 Anna, Year 5, Term 1, 9yrs 9mths

Year 6

Anna's developing confidence as a speller now meant that she no longer relied mainly on phonetic strategies. She was becoming more aware of letter patterns, of how words were structured and the role of meaning in the spelling of words. In discussion with Anna in September she revealed that her command of spoken Italian was now reasonably fluent and that she could read the language but not always understand texts beyond the literal. She continued to read widely in English (authors such as C. S. Lewis and Jean Ure) and this experience was reflected in her writing (see Example 4 and Spelling Assessment).

Anna worked closely with her teacher and found that she benefited from being expected to learn particular groups of words where each group had a detectable common pattern (e.g. -ation). This raised her awareness of analogy-making and improved her spelling knowledge. By the Summer term her standard of writing was generally high and she was able to communicate and organise her ideas clearly. She had an understanding of the various demands of the Key Stage 2 curriculum with regard to writing (e.g. research techniques, scientific investigations, narrative and poetry). At the end of the year the closing gap between her competence as a reader and as a speller is revealed in a practice piece of writing for SATs (see Example 5). However, she still had some way to go before her reading and spelling development could be considered to be on an equal footing.

Summary

Anna was a competent reader and writer and articulate speaker who experienced some difficulty in coming to terms with the English spelling system. She was an almost fluent Italian speaker and could read the language although at a fairly basic level. Since she was eight years old she had continually made comparisons between the English and Italian spelling systems and had at times been very confused about effective and ineffective strategies in the two languages.

Anna loved writing and wrote at length at school and also at home throughout the three years. By Year 6 she wrote longer texts (300+ words at a time) and was a competent writer across a range of topics. She was fully aware of the need to engage the reader.

At the beginning of Year 4 she used a narrow range of spelling strategies, with a particular emphasis

Example 4 Anna, Year 6, Term 1, 10yrs 11mths

Example 5 Anna, Year 6, term 3, 11yrs 4mths

on phonetic strategies. Increasingly in Years 5 and 6, with the help of teachers and other children in the class, she began to look at words with greater intent, to recognise visual patterns and the ways words were structured. By the end of her final year in primary school she usually managed to spell well over 90% of words accurately. Anna's level of achievement as a writer on the Primary Language Record Writing Scales was assessed as Level 4 on Writing Scale 2.

Key elements in supporting Anna's development were:

- The role of teachers in helping her to focus on word patterns and structures. This took place at an individual level and also at a class and group level through word study sessions e.g. prefixes, suffixes, word roots and word origins. She was encouraged to take an interest in how structure and meaning affect spelling.
- The consistent use of a Look–Say–Cover–Write–Check approach when learning new words.
- An emphasis on self-monitoring and on proof-reading, supported by working with editing partners.
- Using a dictionary whenever feasible.
- The fact that her teachers continued to identify significant factors in her development as a speller and to give direct teaching support whenever necessary.
- Her developing awareness of the similarities and differences between spelling in English and Italian, which helped to sharpen her appreciation of where the emphases should lie in learning to spell in English.

CLPE Spelling Assessment Framework

Name *Anna*   Age *10yrs 11mths*   Year group 6   Date/Term *5November, Autumn*

Languages *English/Italian*   Kind of writing *Narrative*

Words spelled in standard form	Structure and Meaning Visual patterns	Phonetic	Early		Pre-linguistic: little understanding of the spelling system
			Phonetic	Visual	
Assessed in detail first 198 words of which 18 were misspelled. *The whole text consisted of 1000 words and overall there were 83 misspellings.*	*slamed* *disition(decision)* *disided* *desided* *where (were)* *(also spelled correctly)* *strait (straight)* *tommorow* *(tomorrow)* *shuters (shutters)*	*carage (carriage)* *- correctly spelled later in text* *libery x 3 (library)* *Isabell (Isobel)* *Kristiner (Kristina)* *horrer (horror)* *curios x 2 (curious)* *befor (before)*			

What does the analysis show about the child's progress in spelling (eg patterns of development)? Note any areas that require particular teaching	
Now over 90% of words spelled in standard form in this extended piece. Her enthusiasm for writing and improving own spelling is considerable - has worked particularly on structural aspects with a good degree of success. Still has difficulty in picking right alternative for a spelling eg uses strait for straight. Needs to continue to use what she does know as basis for spelling new words eg knowledge of word roots and origins eg decide, decision, decide	Total no of words *(assessed)* 198 No of standard spellings *180* % of standard spellings *91%* No of miscues *18* % of miscues *9%*

Spelling Assessment 2 Anna, Year 6, Term 1, 10yrs 11mths

Jonathan: a competent reader and reluctant writer

Year 4–Year 6
Language: English

Year 4

At the beginning of Year 4 Jonathan, a summer-born child, was 8 years 3 months old and described by his teacher as someone whose reading was 'much better than his spelling'. At this point he could tackle short novels but preferred to read information books and poetry. During the year, Jonathan wrote only brief pieces in which there are occasional glimpses of his voice as a writer. His handwriting changed over the year from non-cursive to fully joined, although the script was still very awkward.

An analysis of Jonathan's brief pieces of writing from this year (none more than 75 words long) showed that approximately 80–85% of words were spelled in standard form – mainly familiar words. In spelling words that were unfamiliar to him Jonathan drew on a variety of strategies, often unsuccessfully. With some words – such as *cept* (kept) and *rong* (wrong) – he used a phonetic approach, which seemed inconsistent with the range of words that he could spell correctly. He did not seem to draw on what he knew (see Example 1 and Spelling Assessment 1).

Example 1 and Spelling Asssessment 1 Jonathan, Year 4, Term 1, 8yrs 5mths

Dear David,

How are you? Have you read the intogalactic kichin gose preherstorc If you Havenot there is a littell teddbear calld griff. He got sent to someone calld B.B. Bird. griff coud Fly. Sometimes his circuit went rong and griff went away control. And the Bird tried to stop griff From Flying out of the window. By the way griff was the teddy bear.

from
J

control
circuits

CLPE Spelling Assessment Framework

Name *Jonathan* Age *8yrs 5mths* Year group *4* Date/Term *November, Autumn*

Languages *English* Kind of writing *Letter*

Words spelled in standard form	Structure and Meaning Visual patterns	Phonetic	Early		Pre-linguistic: little understanding of the spelling system
			Phonetic	Visual	
how are *you x 3 have x 2* *read the x 5* *if not* *there is* *a teddy* *bear x 2 griff x 5* *he got* *sent to x 2* *BB Bird x 2* *fly* *sometimes his* *circuit (been corrected)* *went x 2 and x 2* *away* *control (been corrected)* *tried stop* *from x 2 flying* *out of* *window by* *way was* *teddy (been corrected)* *Jonathan*	*intogalactic (intergalactic) preherstorc calld x 2 (called) somo one (someone) coud (could)*	*kichin (kitchen) gose (goes) littell (little) rong (wrong)*			
	What does the analysis show about the child's progress in spelling (eg patterns of development)? Note any areas that require particular teaching *Spelling mostly standard in this short piece. Sometimes relies too much on phonetic strategies in spelling unfamiliar words eg gose littell kichin. Needs help in understanding and working with common prefixes and suffixes eg 'ed' and 'inter'. J. should be encouraged to monitor his own spelling and to work on particular words, and patterns eg 'ould', words beginning with 'wr'.*	Total no of words *67* No of standard spellings *57* % of standard spellings *85%* No of miscues *10* % of miscues *15%*

There were some common visual patterns in his misspellings but his memory of these was often shaky and just 'out' by one or two letters e.g. *coud*. He also needed help in understanding common prefixes and suffixes e.g. *-ed*, *-ing* and *-ly* (see Example 2). Double consonants, as in *shopping* were very often written as single letters. At this stage, Jonathan did not have many self-help strategies: 'If I can't spell a word I put it in my book and go and ask my teacher.' He was unsure about the Look–Say–Cover–Write–Check approach: 'I sometimes use Look–Say–Cover–Write–Check, it works sometimes and not others because I forget the spellings.'

> Our visit to J Sainsburys
> We went to J Sainsburs by
> coach. We left at tea
> o'clock. We got there safelie.
> plus we saw the coach
> driver getana some shopping.
> We met some one coled
> Denise.
> She had a very very
> very very soft voice.
> We went out the back.
> Alex cept gettang in
> peopols way.
> We saw the fish mungers
> & the backery.
> that was at something like
> 11 o'clock.
> Soon it was time to go.

Example 2 Jonathan, Year 4, Term 2, 8yrs 9mths

Year 5

During Year 5, encouraged by his teacher's provision of regular opportunities to write, Jonathan really began to engage with the writing process. He wrote in a wider range of genres and wrote significantly longer pieces (200–300 words on occasion) with far greater confidence and commitment. He wrote freely and did not attempt to confine himself to words he knew how to spell.

Alongside this growing confidence, important developments took place in his spelling during the year. In attempting unfamiliar words, Jonathan made analogies with known words, which reflected his phonetic approach (e.g. drawing on *sandwiches* to write *langwichs* for *languages*). As Jonathan wrote more, the suffixes *-ing* and *-ed* became firmly established. He began to self-correct his own spellings, saying that 'I look up some words in a dictionary and write them on top'. Jonathan was helped by his teacher to list words for spelling practice and to use Look–Say–Cover–Write–Check in this practice more consistently His spelling partner, Alex, played an important role: they read through pieces of each other's work and drew attention to misspellings. Jonathan commented 'We test each other and it helps us remember.' He focused on specific aspects of spelling for practice (e.g. double consonants) and as a result words containing double consonants were increasingly spelled correctly. The rate of misspellings fell from approximately 12% at the beginning of the year to 6% by the end.

Spelling miscues that were phonetic in character still continued to appear in Jonathan's writing e.g. *carstals* for *castles*) but to a lesser extent. Errors were increasingly connected with a developing understanding of the visual and meaning aspects of spelling. For example he wrote *alowed* and *aloud* for *allowed.* (see Example 3 and Spelling Assessment 2). In terms of punctuation, full stops became firmly established and, half way through the year, capitalisation was established. His cursive handwriting became much more fluent.

Example 3 and Spelling Assessment 2
Jonathon, Year 5, Term 2, 9yrs 6mths

CLPE Spelling Assessment Framework

Name *Jonathan*   Age *9yrs 6mths*   Year group 5   Date/Term *January, Spring*

Languages *English*   Kind of writing *Diary*

Words spelled in standard form	Structure and Meaning Visual patterns	Phonetic	Early		Pre-linguistic: little understanding of the spelling system
			Phonetic	Visual	
The x 2 most gift I (x4) ever got Sunday Dear Diary Christmas Eve and can't wait till Maybe sooner x 2 get to sleep the will come etc	*its (it's) bunnys x 2 (bunnies) magnafy (magnify) tightern (tighten) sine (sign) to (too) to (too) fantactic (fantastic) (could be phonetic?) tomorow (tomorrow) x 3 crators (craters) favorite (favourite) startid*	*minits (minutes) dosent (doesn't) shoudon (shouldn't)*			

What does the analysis show about the child's progress in spelling (eg patterns of development)? Note any areas that require particular teaching

J. is writing more freely, with more confidence about what he wants to say. Spellings are almost entirely standard. Misspellings relate mainly to more complex vocabulary and to meaning and strucural areas of spelling eg 'magnafy', 'tightern'. Still occasionally uses phonetic approaches eg 'shoudon' and 'dosent'. J. has clearly benefited from attention to structural elements of spelling - now needs to take on more responsibility for final editing of pieces, including attending to sentence punctuation.

Total no of words *343*

No of standard spellings *325*

% of standard spellings *95%*

No of miscues *18*

% of miscues *5%*

Year 6

During the course of his final year in primary school, Jonathan wrote in an even wider range of genres: a variety of stories, historical accounts, accounts of science experiments, posters, plans, book reviews and letters (see Example 4). His teacher helped the class to develop writing in Science which Jonathan particularly enjoyed. Jonathan still often reverted to phonetic spellings which seemed more reminiscent of an earlier stage (e.g. *bord* for *board*, *sertan* for *certain*, *travald* for *travelled* and *mishon* for *mission*) but, in general, he increasingly made analogies which showed an awareness of visual patterns (e.g. *sighn* for *sign* and *releaf* for *relief*). Sometimes, within the same piece, Jonathan still showed his uncertainty by using different spellings for the same word within a piece of writing e.g. *countury* and *contury* for *country*.

However, he became increasingly able to articulate both his difficulties and the ways in which he was being helped to overcome them. As he stated perceptively 'Words with silent letters give me the most trouble. Sometimes you get muddled up with words like chopped – you don't know whether to put two 'ps' or just one.' (see Example 6). During the year, the Look-Cover-Write-Check approach continued in class, as part of school policy, as did checking with a partner. Jonathan listed and worked on words to be learned on Monday morning and, later in the week, partners tested each other.

Summary

At the beginning of Year 4 Jonathan was a reluctant writer and wrote little. For Jonathan, the increasingly wide range of writing he was encouraged to do from Year 5 onwards, together with teachers' response to him as a writer, played a vital role in promoting his sense of confidence and purpose.

His progress in spelling, from Year 5 onwards, also took place within the strong framework of a whole class approach to working on spelling. Within the classroom spelling was addressed in a variety of ways: whole class sessions which looked at particular aspects of words, group work, individual work on his own spellings, including areas of particular difficulty, and regular practice with a partner.

Particularly significant in Jonathan's development was the role played by teachers in helping him to establish a habit of self-monitoring through correcting his own writing, working with a spelling partner, and deliberately working on aspects of his spelling. All of these approaches were shown to be effective as he

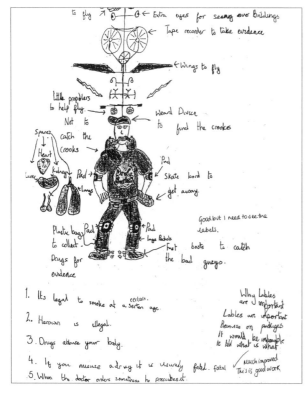

Example 4 Jonathan, Year 6, Term 2, 10yrs 7mths

Example 5 Jonathan, Year 6, Term 2, 10yrs 9mths

became increasingly able to refer to aspects of his own development during the regular conferences.

In the development of his spelling, there was a gradual reduction in the percentage of spelling errors. The quality of his spelling errors also changed noticeably: from phonetic errors to errors which showed much greater awareness of visual patterns and of the meaning and structure of words. Jonathan's level of achievement as a writer on the Primary Language Record Writing Scales was assessed as Level 4 on Writing Scale 2.

Key elements in supporting Jonathan's development

- Being encouraged by teachers to write in a wider range of genres for different purposes e.g. scientific writing, letters, diaries
- Being encouraged to develop habits of self-monitoring through proof reading and editing his work, working with a spelling partner
- His teachers' analysis of his difficulties and strengths; targeted teaching of certain features e.g. words with similar patterns, consonant doubling
- A whole class approach to Look–Say–Cover–Write–Check with time to work on words arising from writing
- Discussion and activities based on aspects of spelling arising from children's writing in a wide range of contexts

Common factors in the development of Anna and Jonathan in Year 4

- Both drew on predominantly phonological strategies when spelling unfamiliar words.
- They tended to see the spelling system as arbitrary as they:
  — spelled the same word in different ways
  — represented the same feature in different ways (they had great difficulty in choosing the correct letter pattern to represent a particular word, e.g. *thort* and *thought*)
  — used letter patterns which didn't exist
  — did not use what they knew (i.e. did not think of a word they could spell to spell an unfamiliar word)
  — sometimes substituted a word which had similar features but the wrong meaning

Common factors which supported their progress in a general sense

- Both Anna and Jonathan were helped by their teachers to help themselves and to become reflective about their own development.
- Their teachers helped them to use their strengths.
- Both children were encouraged to be writers and to write in a range of forms.
- Above all they were helped to see themselves as writers and thinkers and to expand their writing repertoire in spite of their difficulties with spelling. This was important in both cases – but even more so with Jonathan, who was more reluctant to write.

Factors which particularly supported their spelling development

- They were encouraged to take an active role in their own development as spellers and became more reflective, analytical and responsible for their own development.
- They actively edited and self-corrected their writing, including working with a spelling partner.
- They were helped to make connections at many different levels in order to develop their spelling knowledge, e.g. making analogies between words with similar rimes, visual patterns, word structures and meanings.
- Routines such as working with a spelling partner or Look–Say–Cover–Write–Check were given a particular focus (e.g. a particular root word, pattern or structural aspect).
- Word and language study became an important whole class activity – investigations and discussion were an important part of this.

A further feature of the progress of these two children was that, while dependent on a predominantly phonological route into spelling at the early stages, part of their development was the move towards the integration of many different kinds of knowledge, even as they tackled individual words.

Recommendations

Because children like Anna and Jonathan are competent or even highly fluent readers, it is easier for their needs as spellers to be overlooked. If by the age of seven or eight the discrepancy between reading and spelling becomes increasingly marked, then it is necessary not only to identify such children but to provide direct teaching and support. Assessment, using a framework such as the *CLPE Spelling Assessment Framework*, played an important role in identifying areas of their spelling for particular attention. (At the end of this chapter we provide an outline for an Individual Education Programme.)

GOOD READERS AND POOR SPELLERS: ANALYSIS OF COMMON FACTORS AND TEACHING APPROACHES

As Anna and Jonathan were already competent readers when the case studies began we cannot comment on their early reading strategies. What we do know is that when we began to observe them they were able to read a range of texts appropriate for their age – with Anna being the much more avid reader.

Because they did not make many miscues when reading aloud, we can only be tentative about their reading strategies. However, it seemed from errors that Jonathan made when we carried out a Miscue Analysis that he had a tendency to use only partial visual cues with unfamiliar words. For both of these children, who were competent readers by this time, the use of semantic and syntactic cues was sufficiently integrated with their use of visual information to ensure reasonable accuracy for most of the time. Thus when Jonathan read *Martin* for *Martian* and *Julie* for *July* he was concentrating on being accurate, but using only partial cues at the expense of making meaning.

For both Anna and Jonathan, what Uta Frith calls reading by partial cues may have been the preferred option (Frith, 1980). By this Frith means reading which 'capitalises on the redundancy present in written language, in that many elements in a word are not essential to its recognition'. Readers who read in this way are likely to read rapidly, sampling only as much of the print as is necessary to establish the meaning. Such an approach to reading 'would provide less opportunity for acquiring knowledge of the underlying spelling systems.' In other words both Anna and Jonathan, while achieving fluency as readers, did not draw from their reading sufficient awareness of the patterning of words – in particular the visual, structural and semantic aspects. Their sense of how the spelling system was structured therefore remained at an earlier, phonetic stage and they used mainly phonetic approaches in spelling unfamiliar words.

The two children experienced some degree of difficulty in their spelling throughout the three years we worked with them. Initially Anna had quite a large repertoire of known words, and used a very limited approach to spelling unfamiliar words, relying predominantly (but not exclusively) on a phonological route. Jonathan, too, had a well-established vocabulary of words he knew how to spell and used phonologically plausible approximations for unfamiliar words (e.g. *tarachula* [tarantula], *towas* [towers], *toch* [touch]).

This tendency for good readers who are poor spellers to use a phonological approach in spelling is borne out by others who have explored this area. Uta Frith (1980) points out that good readers who are poor spellers (as in the case of Anna and Jonathan) tend to make spelling errors that are phonologically plausible, even though visually unconventional. For example Anna spells *journey* as *gerny* and *turn* as *tern*. Certainly both children stated on many occasions that they 'listened to the sounds in words', this being their main strategy in spelling unfamiliar words.

What this indicates, as a hypothesis, is that good readers who are good spellers utilise a range of different kinds of knowledge gained from their reading and experiences of print. On the other hand children who are good readers but poor spellers probably attend only to partial cues in their reading and in their spelling tend to adopt a mainly phonological approach in attempting to spell unfamiliar words. This is likely to be due to the fact that, as they are paying less attention to the whole of the word, their knowledge of other aspects of spelling is not highly developed.

On the other hand children who are both poor readers and poor spellers, have limited knowledge of the writing system. They therefore have few strategies that they can draw on as both readers and spellers and may be unaware of the most fundamental aspects of the patterning of the writing system. However, all children will exhibit different strengths and weaknesses and must therefore be considered as individuals.

Different relations between reading and spelling

Good readers/good spellers	*Good readers/poor spellers*	*Poor readers/poor spellers*
Become able to integrate many different kinds of knowledge in their reading and spelling – sound, visual, meaning, structural; make links between their reading and spelling	Draw on more limited visual information in reading; rely more heavily on phonological strategies in spelling; don't make links between strategies for reading and those for spelling	Have limited information to draw on from reading; have few effective strategies in spelling – either phonological or visual

DANIEL: A CHILD WITH DIFFICULTIES IN BOTH READING AND SPELLING

Year 3–Year 6
Language: English

Daniel, was not identified as a 'core' case study until Year 5. Then, because his difficulties were proving so significant, we decided to include him as part of our closer study. Daniel's difficulties were such that they could be described as specific learning difficulties or dyslexia. During Year 5, he was put on the Special Needs register. Because of our concern for his development we tracked his progress for a further year into Year 6,

Year 3

At the beginning of Year 3 there were already clear signs that Daniel was finding spelling difficult. Significantly, his progress in reading was also slow: his teacher reported that he was able to read only simpler picture books and reading scheme texts such as the early *Story Chest* books. Daniel did not have any hearing, sight, language or learning difficulties that could explain his problems in the area of literacy.

Over the course of Year 3 Daniel's pieces of writing tended to be very brief (only 35 words on average). As in the case of many spellers who have limited knowledge of the written language system, Daniel had a small bank of words which he knew how to spell. However, he saw these words as individual units, making no link between words that he could write correctly and new words which were similar in some way. This also applied to the spelling of the same word within the same piece. For example in one short piece he wrote *aatec* and *atw* for *attic* within 2 lines (see Example 1 and Spelling Assessment1).

Many of Daniel's spellings seemed to be strongly influenced by the idiosyncratic way he pronounced words slowly to himself as he wrote and represented them by letters (e.g. *fuou* for *view*). The fact that he constantly changed the ways he represented particular sounds demonstrated the difficulties he was having with the spelling system. In some cases he did not manage to identify the main sounds in words,

---

CLPE Spelling Assessment Framework

Name *Daniel*   Age *7yrs 8mths*   Year group *3*   Date/Term *September, Autumn*

Languages *English*   Kind of writing *Brief reflective piece*

Words spelled in standard form	Structure and Meaning Visual patterns	Phonetic	Early		Pre-linguistic: little understanding of the spelling system
			Phonetic	Visual	
my x 2 is I and it x 2 me a my has	becus (because) papar (paper)	fuou (view) faratt (favourite) pas (place) aatec (attic) lic (like) hiais (heights) gafs (gives) god (good)	licke (like) lioks (looks) wal (wall)	swtcolncon (partly phonetic as well? be fro (before) goon (gone)	atw (attic) tat (turtle)

What does the analysis show about the child's progress in spelling (eg patterns of development)? Note any areas that require particular teaching

D. is at the very early stages of literacy learning: his spelling knowledge is still at a very basic stage. Has a small core of known words and knows most initial sounds and usually picks out other predominant consonants in his spelling. He uses mostly phonetic strategies but also visual sometimes, but all at very early stage, where he is making very little connection between spelling of one word and another eg spells 'like' differently.

Need to continue to boost confidence in himself as a writer – and to help him build up a vocabulary of known words. From this list identify any common letter patterns.

Total no of words *26*

No of standard spellings *11*

% of standard spellings *42%*

No of miscues *15*

% of miscues *58%*

Spelling Assessment 1 Daniel, Year 3, Term 1, 7yrs 8mths

nor did he have a visual idea of the word. In some instances words were miscopied.

His teacher's initial strategy was to write out Daniel's pieces again, spelled in standard form, without focusing on misspellings. While this is a common approach used by teachers for children at the early stages of spelling, it was not enough to give Daniel the support he needed (see Example 2).

There was no doubt that Daniel did feel that he could put down his ideas in writing: he stated repeatedly that this was the most important thing – 'to get my ideas down'. His writing showed that he certainly did not restrict his writing to words he knew how to spell. Unfortunately, however, when he did go back to his spellings, he had few strategies for self-correction. 'I have to try and do it and it's hard to find the letters. I start with the first letter and sound the word out', he commented. Over the year between 30–60% of words written were non-standard and most of these misspellings fell into the 'Early phonetic' category, with many other words categorised on the Spelling Assessment Framework as 'words which showed little understanding of the spelling' e.g. *8 ur onss* for *8 year olds*.

My Favrott Pas
is my aatbec Becus
I lic hiais and Ib
Gaes me a Good Flou.
My atiU lioks Like
it has tatt WaU papar

My favourite place is my attic, because I like heights and it gives me a good view. My attic looks like it has turtle wallpaper.

Example 1 Daniel, Year 3, Term 1, 7yrs 8mths

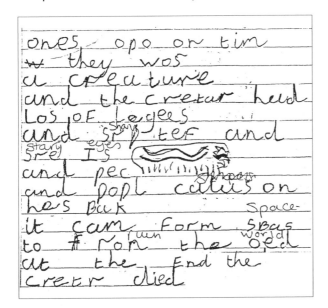

Ones opo on tim
they wos
a creature
and the cretar had
Los oF Legees
and sray ter and
srey I's
and pec
and popl caus on
he's Bck
it cam Form sbas
to From the oed
at the End the
cretr died

Once upon a time there was a creature and creature had lots of eyes and sharp teeth and starey eyes and pink and purple colours on his back it came from space to run the world at the end the creature died

Example 2 Daniel, Year 3, Term 3, 8yrs 5mths

Year 4

During this year, Daniel's written texts grew slightly longer – 50 words on average over the year. His handwriting became clear, well formed, joined and fluent. However, his major strategy for spelling remained unchanged: trying to represent sounds he could hear in words, without any systematic approach to the spelling system. The extent to which this strategy became misleading is shown at one point when he even began to add -ar to the ends of particular words ending in a consonant e.g. *logar* for *long*, *wosar* for *was* – again reflecting the particular way he said words aloud to himself while writing them (see Example 3).

Once again his teacher's main strategy was to write out the piece in standard form at the bottom of the piece and to discuss with Daniel as she did so. She also began to circle spellings to be worked on (usually commonly occurring words which Daniel had misspelled). One of the pieces in which his spelling was most successful was a piece of dictation taken from a book he had been reading. The teacher circled some of the misspellings and listed those to be worked on at the end. Alongside the other more adventurous kinds of writing, this kind of activity was helpful in allowing him to focus closely on writing down words which he had already seen in the meaningful context of a known book.

It was also clear, for example, that Daniel had been working on *-ing*. In some notes he writes in a science topic *-ing* is used correctly many times, although the remainder of the word is not in standard form. In general, making systematic collections of words with particular letter patterns would have been helpful in helping to make aspects of the spelling system more explicit to Daniel, and in helping him to use analogies to attempt new words.

A long time ago in South Africa there was lots of wars and some people got killed in the wars and lots of people got taken to cells Then Nelson Mandela took over and said black people and white people get on the same basis and thats how nowadays its different

Example 3 Daniel, Year 4, Term 1, 8yrs 9mths

Year 5

Year 5 saw a significant shift in Daniel's development as a writer. He wrote more frequently, in a greater variety of genres and at much greater length: accounts, book reviews, retellings of myths and stories, information writing, poetry and his own stories. His written texts grew rapidly in length – an average of 155 words, with two or three pieces of 300–400 words. A significantly growing number of familiar words were spelled in standard form and Daniel's misspellings dropped from 30–40% at the beginning of the year to 20–30% by the end. During this year, Daniel began to use full stops more consistently and to experiment with other forms of punctuation such as speech marks and exclamation marks.

However there were still great concerns over his spelling. Significantly early in the year, there were still many occasions when Daniel did not recognise where one word ended and another began e.g. *trime* for *try me* and there were occasions where he still spelled the same word in different ways within the same piece. He was also unaware of the ending *-ed* – using *t*, *it* and *et* at the ends of past tense verbs. He continued to write a variety of spellings of the same word within the same piece e.g. *whiv*, *wev* and *weeth* for *with*. Daniel had also developed his own ways of representing sounds – for *ch*, *sh* and *ti* (as in *-tion*) Daniel used *c* e.g. *cicin* for *chicken*, *copatecon* for *competition* (see Example 4).

By the end of Year 5 Daniel was able to explain that he was aware that a word was always spelled the same each time, but, 'when it was in rough, I spelled it different ways because I didn't really bother to look'. He also explained how he went about spelling: 'I try and make it sound (the word) but I do it quickly before I forget my ideas.' He added 'I try and go a bit more slowly now.' His teacher supported Daniel's spelling development in different ways. She identified common words that were misspelled in his writing, listing them at the side, and identifying those for practice using Look–Say–

on the way to KFC (Kentucky Fried Chicken) I can nearly taste the chicken as it melts in my mouth I walk through the door I see sweetcorn melting in butter I get my food and I find a seat I get a piece of chicken out the bucket and I am licking my lips I have another bit it's delicious I say but before I know it's gone time for the lovely sweetcorn I have a bit it's so lovely I'm scoffing it in but it's gone I go home licking my lips

Example 4 Daniel, Year 5, Term 1, 9yrs 8mths

CLPE Spelling Assessment Framework

Name *Daniel* Age *9yrs 8mths* Year group 5 Date/Term *October, Autumn*

Languages *English* Kind of writing *Descriptive writing*

Words spelled in standard form	Structure and Meaning Visual patterns	Phonetic	Early		Pre-linguistic: little understanding of the spelling system
			Phonetic	Visual	
on the x 6 way to KFc I x 14 as it x3 in x 3 my x 4 door get x 3 food and x 3 a x 4 of x 2 out am have x3 bit x 3 say x2 to but x2 time for am so go home	befro no (know) it x 4 (it's) Im (I'm)	cun (can) malt (melt) mafa (pronunciation) batar (butter) set (seat) bacit a navar x 2 (another) lavley (lovely) seetcon (sweetcorn) lavey (lovely) gun(gone) leps (lips)	nley (nearly) tat (taste) wooc (walk) troow (through) matin (melting) pecs (piece) cicin (chicken) leecin (licking) leepss (lips) dlsh (delicious) delsh (delicious) my shf (myself)	swtcolncon (partly phonetic as well?) be fro (before) goon (gone)	cein (chicken) shie (see) soofin (scoffing) lein (licking)

What does the analysis show about the child's progress in spelling (eg patterns of development)?
Note any areas that require particular teaching
D is writing at greater length and has increased the percentage of words spelled in standard form by approximately 20% since last year. However, his strategies - mostly phonetic - remain very ineffective. He continues to spell the same word in different ways eg 'cein' and 'cicin' for chicken, 'leps' and 'leepss' for lips.

Work on one or two familiar words eg can and lips, and help D to create new words using different onsets.
Work on suffix 'ing' - make a collection of words.
Encourage D to look at words within words eg my-self.

Total no of words 108

No of standard spellings 68

% of standard spellings 63%

No of miscues 40

% of miscues 37%

Spelling Assessment 1 Daniel, Year 5, Term 1, 9yrs 8mths

Cover–Write–Check. She also encouraged him to practise words containing common letter patterns such as ee and ea and in class writing sessions his teacher drew on children's writing to focus on aspects of spelling such as the -ed ending.

There is no doubt that Daniel's growing ability to write at length, and the way in which he was bravely prepared to tackle the spelling of a wide range of new vocabulary, were positive aspects of his development. It meant, however, that his difficulties were more sharply exposed than if he had restricted himself to a narrower range of writing.

By the Spring term, there were small but significant signs of progress (see Example 5). When Daniel copied words such as *Hades* or *Persephone*, they were more often correctly spelled; the number of known words grew significantly; in some words, visual letter patterns such as *ck* and *ch* began to be represented – although sometimes they were used incorrectly; the *-ed* ending became established. In addition, Daniel's awareness of syllabification in words had improved – for example he spelled *pomegranate* as *poneitgrampit*. Previously, there had sometimes been little evidence of even this most basic element of phonological awareness in his spelling of unfamiliar words.

In general a higher proportion of familiar words were spelled in standard form, although the rate of misspellings tended to increase with the intensity of his involvement with a particular piece. For example in the first draft of a beautifully expressive poem 'In My View' (see Example 6 – final draft) which Daniel wrote during the Summer term, there was a higher rate of misspellings than in other pieces. Despite the existence of many more words in standard form, Daniel still reverted to highly implausible attempts such as *orindcng* for *ordinary*.

At the end of year 4, Daniel had been reading very slowly; he stopped at every word. By the end of this year he was beginning to self-correct in reading, scanning back over the text to re-read a sentence to establish meaning and was beginning to use grapho-phonic cues more confidently, breaking unfamiliar words into chunks.

It was a hot day and persephone goes over to the shade and she puts her hands in the water to cool them Down and suddenly she thinks someone is watching her and she gets a tingle in her back and ran off. So Hades the god of the underground went to Zeus and said I've fallen in love with persephone and I want to marry her So Zeus couldn't say no but he couldn't say yes. because his wife would cry and he didn't want the crops to die the next day persephone was sitting on the hill she was picking some petals when the earth started to crumble she didn't know what was happening and just then Hades came out the underground in a chariot with 4 black horses pulling it. and they took her when persephone's mum found out abour her instead of wearing bright ordinary clothes she wore dull black clothes and she was falling around for 9 days without food and drink. And she never made anything grow for 9 days … (Extract)

Example 5 Daniel, Year 5, Term 2, 10yrs 1mth

Example 6 Daniel, Year 5, Term 3

Postscript: Year 6

Because of our concern for Daniel's progress we carried out a further collection of his writing in Year 6 and sampled his reading once more. His reading – of a scheme text with several lines of text to a page – was becoming more fluent. He still tended to read word by word but had speeded up considerably, and he was also reading parts of words in 'chunks' for example *shop-ping*. He also self-corrected and, on occasions, scanned over the text to predict or confirm words he was unsure of.

Daniel had continued to write at length, often working with his writing partner, Kimberley. 'I like to write a lot. We have to make it interesting for a reader. My teacher says "It won't just be you that's going to read it but your writing partner, your parents … and even your grandchildren!"' There had also been further developments in Daniel's spelling. The number of words he knew how to spell had increased, as had the proportion of misspellings. These now tended to fall into the structural, semantic and visual categories when analysed with the Spelling Assessment Framework, rather than being almost entirely phonetic as in previous years (see Example 7 and Spelling Assessment 2). Attempts at words reflected visual patterns, e.g. *woak* (*woke*) and *sean* (*scene*) or structural features, e.g. *comeing* (*coming*) and *sadily* (*sadly*). No words fell into the early phonetic categories and those which fell into the phonetic category were plausible (e.g. *thort* for *thought*, *hapend* for *happened*).

When asked how he had known to spell *night,* Daniel remarked, 'It's easy, I just think how to spell *light*.' Daniel was developing a sense of all aspects of the spelling system. When asked what had made him better at spelling, Daniel replied, 'The fact I need to do it – it's important, and it makes me more determined.' His Year 6 teacher confirmed that Daniel had developed in all areas that year, improving in confidence. His competency in maths and numeracy had also developed well.

Summary

In Year 3, Daniel's understanding of the spelling system was very limited; his reading was also at the early stages – *Level 1, inexperienced reader* on the Primary Language Record Reading Scale 2. In the early stages teachers tried to support his development by encouraging him to write and take a full part in the curriculum. More particularly they intervened by writing out his text in standard form underneath and identifying common words for him to practise. He was also supported by some phonics work. However, the extent of his continuing difficulties meant that a more analytical and systematic approach would have been more helpful, e.g. word building activities which drew attention first to the phonetic aspects and later the visual patterning of the system.

Plan

(1) Set in 1997	(6) Jo has a favourite tree
(2) a dog and owner.	(7) a rescue service fail to rescue
(3) they both die and get buried	(8) adverbs
(4) dog name is Jim	(9) golden phrases
(5) owner's name is Jo	(10) colourful words

It is 1997 and Jo has Just woke up in a fright his face was soaking wet as someone that's Just came out of a pool. Just then his dog came in the room "hi Jim" said Jo calmly "are you coming for walkies" he said excitedly.

The dog was excited Jo could see it in his eyes Woof the dog went suddenly. Jo got dressed and thought that he would go to his favourite tree. By then Jo's tummy rumbled it was 8.00 time for him and his dog's breakfast. When they finished their breakfast they went to the park.

(Extract from 295 words)

Example 7 and Spelling Assessment 2
Daniel, Year 6, Term 2, 11yrs 3mths

CLPE Spelling Assessment Framework

Name *Daniel*   Age *11yrs 3mths*   Year group 6   Date/Term *April, Spring*

Languages *English*   Kind of writing *Story narrative*

Words spelled in standard form	Structure and Meaning Visual patterns		Phonetic		Early		Pre-linguistic: little understand-ing of the spelling system
					Phonetic	Visual	
It	walk-	oaner x 3	mutch	resku (x2)	past(passed)			exisenthy
is came	ies	(owner)	to (too)	sirveais	freasean			(excitedly)
and out	he x2	addvirbs	sadily (sadly)	(service)	(freezing)			brikg (brekfast)
Jo x4 of	was	goulden	puled (pulled)	boaf (both)	eminjinse			alod (an old?)
has pool	could	couleuful	sliped	baryed	(emergency)			
just then	see	woak (woke)	masive sweped	(x)(buried)	sirves x3			
x3 dogx3	it	fight (fright)	(swept)	faveart x3	woere x6			
up came	went	thats (that's)	ceped (kept)	frases	shoked			
inx3 thex3	got	comeing	dreem	(phrases)	(shocked)			
a x2 room	and	eaixstighted	(dream)	carmily x2	walter x4			
his x3 hi	that	(excited)	sean (scene)	eys (eyes)	bolding			
face Jim	tree	sudenly	fail (fell)	wof	(building)			
was saidx2	etc	there (their)	throw x2	drest	fau (few)			
as x2 are		could (cold)	(through)	thort x2	minits			
wet you		(slipped)	croud x2	woold	resku			
some- for		(massive)	befour	(would)	carent			
one		throwx2	puch (push)	tamy	(current)			
		mobail	bubles	(tummy)	vaiently (?)			
		(mobile) x 2	braking	rombled	sain (?)			
		painick(panic)	reeds (reads)	brikfist	ded			
		sean (scene)	loveing	hapend x3	arftar			
		witch (which)	(loving)	wen	hart.....etc			

What does the analysis show about the child's progress in spelling (eg patterns of development)?
Note any areas that require particular teaching

Daniel continues to write relatively confidently – does not restrict his writing to familiar words.
Important signs of development are: a growing number of common words spelled correctly; a growing consistency with both standard spellings and his misspellings (before would spell words in several different ways at times). Although the greater proportion of his misspellings are probably phonetic, a growing number of misspellings contain visual patterns or are linked to structural or meaning errors. Many more of his misspellings show that he is beginning to catch on to the spelling system.

- *look at suffixes -ing, -ed, and -ly if appropriate – Daniel is probably in a position to now to begin to take on these aspects.*
- *familiar words – look say cover write check with there, were, would/could, water and high interest words like emergency*
- *help him to see words within words eg break-fast*

Total no of words 295

No of standard spellings 224

% of standard spellings 76%

No of miscues 71

% of miscues 24%

As Daniel entered year 5 his difficulties were perceived to be very great. However, the school had little resources for extra teaching or support, even though Daniel was put on Stage 2 of the Code of Practice. Analysis using the CLPE Spelling Assessment Framework helped his teacher in Year 5 to identify particular aspects of development which Daniel needed to address. In addition, she encouraged him to work more systematically on misspellings identified in his writing, working with a spelling partner. Throughout, Daniel was encouraged to see himself as a writer – this was paramount. Despite his difficulties, support from teachers and his involvement in the project made him more reflective about his spelling – he moved from 'hearing sounds' and 'getting words down' to considering how he needed to 'take things more slowly' and to work on his spellings using Look–Say–Cover–Write–Check. It is also significant that development in reading and in spelling went hand in hand – each supporting the other.

Finally, it is apparent that in Year 6, he began to demonstrate a much wider understanding of the spelling system and awareness of himself as a speller, creating hypotheses which drew much more on the visual aspects of spelling, word structures and meanings. Over the four years he moved from Level 1 on PLR Writing Scale 2 to Level 3 and gained a Level 3 in SATS at the end of Year 6.

Because Daniel was the only case study child who experienced such difficulties in both reading and spelling, it is impossible to draw general conclusions from his experience. However, it is important to summarise key elements which supported his development.

Key elements in supporting Daniel's development

General factors

- Daniel was always helped to see himself as a writer, including at the problematic early stages when his understanding of the spelling system was very limited.
- He was encouraged to write in a range of forms and increasingly at greater length.
- Daniel took a full part in the curriculum despite his difficulties in reading and spelling.
- Daniel was increasingly encouraged by teachers, particularly from year 5 onwards, to become more reflective about his spelling through discussing strategies and to take some responsibility for his own development (i.e. through working on his spellings, discussing with a partner).

Spelling: early stages

At the early stages, when Daniel was also having difficulties with reading, it was true to say that his difficulties proved problematic for teachers. Strategies which could have supported Daniel's development further were:

- use of the Spelling Assessment Framework to identify particular patterns, known words for practice and to establish his level of spelling knowledge;
- helping him to syllabify words;
- discussion of his strategies – e.g. helping him to look at words, rather than just to 'sound them out';
- greater attention to word-building, using onset and rime approaches;
- listing words that he could successfully spell.

Spelling: later stages

Approaches adopted by Daniel's teachers in Years 5 and 6 were particularly important. During this period Daniel grew in confidence and experience as a reader. He was then able to draw on a much wider experience of words and their visual forms, from which he made generalisations and analogies.

Particularly helpful approaches were:

- practice of commonly occurring words, letter patterns, and word structures arising in his writing;

- encouragement of analogy-making, e.g. 'You've used "ed" here, let's see how many other words we can think of/write using the same ending/pattern';
- word building including initial blends, common letter patterns, common suffixes, e.g. *-ed, -ly*;
- use of Look–Say–Cover–Write–Check to practise words arising in his writing; practice with a friendly spelling partner;
- class and group word study sessions where particular features of spelling were investigated and discussed;
- when writing longer pieces, it was important for Daniel to sit with the teacher and work on at least a section of the piece, carefully looking at misspellings and articulating ways of remembering them;
- a personal spelling book of words he could spell, including those with similar patterns.

Conclusions

It is important to note that in all three case studies of children experiencing difficulties, their teachers' role in supporting them as writers was a key factor. All three children thought that it was important to write and continued to grow and develop as writers over the years of the project. The three children all received specific support to some degree from their class teachers – who also had the needs of over thirty other children to consider at the same time, a few of whom had even more significant literacy or learning difficulties. However, as teachers engaged with the spelling project they grew to understand the role of the CLPE Spelling Assessment Framework for diagnostic and monitoring purposes. In particular, the framework helped to identify particular teaching points which were appropriate to particular stages.

In all cases therefore, targeted support made a difference, and could have made an even more significant contribution at an earlier stage. What is important, particularly for children who seem to be performing satisfactorily as readers, is that the discrepancy with their spelling development is recognised and acted upon. The approach outlined opposite may help schools to plan early and appropriate support for children with spelling difficulties.

In the following chapter, we provide a map of significant teaching approaches which, used systematically can support children's progress and development in spelling.

Individual approaches for children with spelling difficulties

Observation and analysis

- Observations of the child writing in the classroom over time
- Collection of a range of writing samples over time
- Frequent discussion with the child about developing strategies
- Analysis of spelling strategies using Spelling Assessment Framework
- Is the child's competence in reading similar to her/his competence as a speller?
- Analysis of child's strategies as a reader using a Running Record or Miscue Analysis may provide more detail

Analysis of strengths and weaknesses

- Identify effective strategies e.g. known words, evidence of consistency in spelling particular words even if not in standard form
- Are the child's strategies predominantly visual, phonically based, or are there other kinds of patterns e.g. reversals, perseveration, errors associated with word structures and meanings?

Child's view of themselves as a writer/speller

- Consider the child's developing confidence, independence, and experience as a writer, their knowledge and understanding, and their ability to reflect on their strategies, as a basis for understanding their view of themselves as a learner
- Consider ways of helping the child to help themselves

Review plans and interventions regularly

What have been the successful learning outcomes?
What aspects need to be worked on and what routines and approaches will support further development?

Drawing up an action plan

On the basis of your observations, analysis and discussion with the child:
- Identify regular routines and approaches to spelling to support development e.g. proof reading, identifying own errors, Look–Say–Cover–Write–Check
- Identify one or two specific teaching points to act on e.g. rhyming words, working with a particular letter pattern

Chapter 6

The effective teaching of spelling

This chapter highlights the most significant kinds of teaching in the three project schools that helped children to move forward in their spelling development. At the end of the chapter there is a section listing recommended teaching approaches for children at Key Stage 1 and Key Stage 2. These teaching approaches were drawn from those observed during the project. Later, they were compiled as guidelines for teaching spelling in the three schools, and have been developed further for the purposes of this book.

TEACHING SPELLING: KEY FINDINGS FROM THE PROJECT

The role of the teacher

One of the most striking findings from the project was the crucial role that certain teachers played in moving children on as spellers. These teachers recognised what individual and groups of children needed and translated their understandings into effective teaching approaches and patterns of classroom organisation. In particular they:

- appreciated that the teaching of spelling involved direct teaching and extended far beyond giving out lists of spellings and intervening in children's writing (although the latter continued to be a key site for teaching);
- combined high expectations of children with approaches that supported them at key learning points;
- promoted very significantly the active involvement of children in their own learning through regular writing conferences, the setting up of spelling and writing partnerships in their classrooms and the promotion of active and investigative approaches to spelling and word study.

Drawing on many sources of knowledge: implications for teaching

In Chapter 3, we concluded from analysis of our case studies that children learning to spell draw on different sources of knowledge, even early on in their development and also that they had different preferences as spellers as they started to spell words. Although many young children took a mainly auditory route into spelling – translating speech sounds into letters – some attended more closely to visual features, and wrote down what they could remember of how a word looks. For children to become successful as spellers however, 'auditory' spellers had to take on the visual aspects of the spelling system and 'visual' spellers needed to develop and refine their understanding of sound/letter relationships.

These findings have important implications for teaching: it seems important that as soon as children begin to tackle the written code, they are encouraged to draw on different kinds of knowledge in their spelling.

At earlier stages children therefore need:

- to encounter written language – through a growing familiarity with texts of all kinds, including environmental print;
- to develop levels of phonological awareness which allow them to analyse sounds in speech;

- to develop their knowledge of letters of the alphabet, learn letter names, and discover how letters are formed in writing;
- to draw on what they know as they learn to link sounds with letters and combinations of letters;
- to develop a sense of the patterns to be found in spelling and to begin to make analogies – using what they know to spell new words.

From our case studies it seemed apparent that children developed these different areas of knowledge not only through teachers' demonstrations (e.g. in shared writing and word study investigations) and through other forms of direct teaching, but also from a wide range of other significant literacy experiences and teaching routines. These extended from children writing their own texts (in contexts such as informal play and role play) to more formally structured writing activities. Activities such as singing songs and rhymes, reading and re-reading texts, and spelling and word games all contributed to children's spelling knowledge.

The following comments from a Reception teacher reflect the variety of teaching approaches:

> In shared writing we talk about initial letters, last letters, referring to an alphabet board. We also work at building up a small bank of words that are used frequently by the children.
>
> I explicitly encourage the children to find and use words – in their writing – that are on display, both commonly used words and more specifically, topicbased words -for example words from a core book like *Mr Gumpy's Outing*.
>
> Children of this age often know letter names and initial sounds but cannot always represent them in symbolic form. So when we practise handwriting together, as I write on the board, we say all the letter names as they are written.
>
> We sing alphabet songs. I ask children to come and point to a letter they know and follow that up by finding out if they know any more words beginning with that letter. We write these chosen words on the board together.
>
> All the children have 'name cards'. I use these in a number of ways, for example, for recognising their name and names of other class members, for identifying differences and similarities in these names.

Later spelling development

As children developed as spellers, particularly at Key Stage 2, other aspects of spelling knowledge became increasingly important. Added to a developing sense of pattern was the importance of children knowing which pattern was most likely and their ability to connect knowledge of a particular pattern to a word meaning i.e., choosing between between *main* and *mane*. Children who were fluent readers but poor spellers found this particularly problematic and benefited from some direct teaching of spelling patterns. Children also needed to attend to the structural and semantic aspects of spelling (e.g. verb endings such as *-ed*, common suffixes such as *-ly* or prefixes such as *inter-*).

Teachers often commented that children's misspellings in their writing failed to reflect spelling teaching – but this kind of comment seemed to relate above all to arbitrary spelling lists and spelling exercises. Children learned spellings most effectively when the focuses for spelling teaching were linked to their writing. Where teachers were intervening effectively in children's writing and discussing with them points that they could work on, children were able to consolidate their spelling knowledge.

For example a teacher would identify a particular area of spelling needing attention – such as *-ed* endings or consonant doubling as in *shopping, hopping* – and encourage the child to work on this in the following weeks, sometimes with a spelling partner. Some teachers then translated points arising from children's writing into topics for group and whole class teaching.

Spelling and reading

Children who were developing early competence as spellers were also developing fluency as readers and seemed to take a particular interest in words. This general interest in language also seemed to be reflected in the way these children began to 'write like readers'. An interest in words themselves, as

This reception class is engaged in shared reading of a big book, *Who's in the Shed?* Shared reading is followed by shared writing, using the book as a model. Children contribute to the writing and the teacher demonstates how the writing goes.

well as an ability to remember spellings, seemed to be a hallmark of these early competent spellers.

We found some evidence of a connection between children's approaches to decoding (reading the print) and encoding (spelling). Children with different learning styles demonstrated different competences at the earliest stages of their spelling development. It seemed likely that these differences also reflected their different perceptions of the reading process.

In the case of children who were developing along a mainly phonological route, there was a clear link between their growing spelling abilities and their growing phonemic awareness. These children were developing an ability to represent every sound in a word, phonetically. This seemed to be linked to their predominantly phonic approach to reading. For spellers with a more visual approach to spelling, reading may have been influencing spelling in different ways. These children tended to notice different features of words – such as the overall shape and length of a word, or letter patterns such as -ed or -ck, which tended to appear early on in their spelling.

However, the children who were at least reasonably fluent (although not necessarily avid) readers but who were poor spellers certainly did not 'pick up' spelling from their reading but needed much more help in acquiring a sense of the patterning of the English spelling system, and a particular emphasis on its visual aspects.

What this means for teaching is that children with very different learning styles in spelling all benefit from reading. All gain from access to a wide range of reading experiences, including shared reading, where teachers talk about features of words – including their spellings and meanings. However, teachers need to be aware of the different aspects of print which children are noticing and help them to consolidate their strengths, as well as to take on new strategies. In addition it is important that different kinds of teaching – both direct and indirect – are provided for those children who are not making links between the words they read and the way these words are spelled.

Shared writing and the role of teacher demonstrations

Shared writing was used by teachers in the study for many purposes and was a key context for teaching all aspects of writing and spelling. During shared writing children had the opportunity to see an experienced writer (the teacher) constructing texts to which they contributed in terms of both composition and transcription. Teachers were able to focus on many different aspects of spelling – rhyming patterns, letter strings, the spelling of whole words, grammatical aspects of spelling and word meanings – alongside other features of writing, according to the age and experience of the class.

> I plan a series of writing activities based on a particular core book such as *The Shopping Basket* – a story map, a letter, a retelling of the story. Firstly I demonstrate the writing through shared writing – everyone offers their ideas for both composing the piece and for spelling and punctuation – then the children are really clear about what I want them to do.
>
> For example when we drew the story map of *The Shopping Basket* I wrote a caption for each scene. I invited children to contribute to the captions. I asked some children to provide initial letters, others to spell parts of a word, others to spell whole words – particularly in the case of high frequency words. I helped children to identify sounds they could hear in words. In some instances I drew attention to common letter patterns as we went along.
>
> (Year 1 teacher)

Occasionally, for very inexperienced writers, teachers scribed for them which played a valuable part in showing how written language was written down.

In general shared writing was much more evident at Key Stage 1 than Key Stage 2. However, teacher demonstrations continued to be highly significant here (where they occurred), whether in demonstrating how new kinds of texts 'worked' or in looking at spelling, punctuation and grammatical features. Shared writing was used to draw attention to rules and generalisations, or to the particular ways words were used in particular kinds of writing.

For example, a Year 5 teacher drew together her class at the end of a writing session. The class had been writing football stories and the teacher helped them to brainstorm a range of words to substitute for kicked. As she recorded the words – *volleyed, blasted, chipped* – the teacher drew attention to the -*ed* endings and consonant doubling. The class were completely engaged as aspects of spelling were being taught in such a high-interest context.

Frequent opportunities to write

In the spelling project there was a considerable variation between classes in the amount, range and depth of writing which children were involved in, across both Key Stages. It is not possible to demonstrate conclusively that all children who had opportunities to write regularly in a wide range of genres, and who had the support of strong models in terms of texts and teacher demonstrations, developed more successfully as spellers. However, it is possible to say on the basis of the case study evidence, that when children were initially denied such opportunities, but later moved to classrooms where these existed, they began to flourish as both writers and spellers. This was the case with regard to children at all ages and levels of experience. In the case of one child with spelling difficulties, the average length of his written pieces rose from 49 words in Year 4 to 155 words in Year 5. Significantly his spelling also began to improve during the same year.

During the spelling project it became apparent that teachers, particularly at Key Stage 2, were finding it more difficult to create time for children to write at length or in depth, due to the demands of the curriculum. Many teachers successfully incorporated a range of opportunities for writing into topics linked to history, science and geography but writing where literary texts provided the focus, or where children were using writing to develop their thinking, seemed to be in short supply. It seemed increasingly the case that writing was seen by teachers (with some exceptions) as the production of short one-off pieces – both narrative and nonnarrative.

However, where the range, length and depth of children's writing was extended it seemed to prove significant in terms of their spelling development. Children's developing competence as spellers generally went alongside the development of their writing in other ways – for example it seemed to be linked to the opportunity to write at greater length, to widen their range of writing, or to use writing for their own thinking. If writing was confined to narrow exercises, then children simply did not have enough opportunities to engage with the spelling of a widening repertoire of words. In some instances case study children's spelling development actually faltered or regressed if their writing was too narrowly focused.

Writing workshops

In some classrooms, a writing workshop approach to spelling was adopted. This offered systematic opportunities for discussing all aspects of the writing process. Writing workshops usually began with shared reading or writing and this time was frequently used to discuss aspects of the writing process, such as planning, revising, editing, spelling, structure and punctuation. Children then worked in groups and the teacher was able to work with specific groups of children. At the end the teacher conducted a short plenary session where excerpts of work in progress were read, and discussed.

This approach was very supportive for both teaching and learning because it offered frequent opportunities for talking about the spelling of words during the actual process of writing. Issues could be addressed at class, group and individual levels. Teaching about spelling was strongly contextualised. The regular conferences with groups offered structured opportunities for working with groups of children so that the teacher could observe, intervene in and discuss children's spelling strategies.

'Having a go'

A frequently discussed question amongst teachers was the issue of letting children 'have a go' with spelling and how and when to offer appropriate support.

While the three spelling project schools had different approaches to the teaching of writing, all teachers working in Reception, Year 1 and 2 classes, with one or two exceptions, encouraged young children to attempt their own spellings. There was a strong belief that doing so was an integral part of the learning process and helped children to make sense of the spelling system. In classrooms where there was a climate of greater dependency – where children relied on adults and word books for almost

every word – children wrote less and it was difficult for teachers to have any significant understanding of where children were in their development or of potential teaching points.

In most classes 'having a go' did not mean that children were unsupported in their spelling. They were supported in many ways. At the early stages some teachers scribed for children when they were reluctant to set pencil to paper. The most important factor seemed to be a classroom ethos where children were encouraged to attempt unfamiliar words, using what they could hear, or remember visually. At the same time teachers drew attention to words from favourite books and topics by putting up charts and posters – children were encouraged to refer to these during writing. Cards with the letters of the alphabet were put on tables and children developed a core of common words which they knew how to spell. As soon as children had begun to 'catch on' to the spelling system, teachers helped them to attend to the standard spelling of those words which they had spelled almost correctly.

By Year 1 some children were being encouraged to look through their writing, identify words where they were unsure of the spelling and look them up in a dictionary. Further support was offered at this stage by having early dictionaries and word banks of common words available on tables.

In Key Stage 2 (children aged 7–11), most teachers in the project schools encouraged children to write freely in the first instance and then to return to spelling and punctuation at a later editing stage; some children used dictionaries as they went along. Children were expected to a greater extent than in Key Stage 1 to use dictionaries, personal word books, thesauruses and other classroom resources either during or after composing. The listing of specialist vocabulary to form a word bank for a new class topic was useful, in that it involved children in discussing new spellings. Teacher intervention and their skill in setting up ways for children to become self-supporting and self-monitoring were important at this stage. Children with special needs were helped by writing down words they could spell in a personal dictionary or on index cards.

Self-awareness and self-monitoring in spelling

Editing and proofreading can begin in KS1. Teachers and children need to be clear about the routines in use in the classroom, and how children are expected to check through their own work. Demonstrations are needed, as part of shared writing sessions, in which the teacher models ways of identifying misspellings (for instance by circling or underlining words).

After misspellings have been identified, there also needs to be a clear routine for children to follow in locating correct spellings. Often this will involve the use of spelling partners or writing partners; children can learn to work effectively together on spellings, using the resources in the classroom. They will need to be particularly confident in the use of a dictionary, and this is a skill which needs to be directly taught. Once these resources have been tried, problems can be brought to a class session or to teachers. In some classrooms, an editing table is set up where some children work as editors with others. In general collaborative working is an effective way of getting children to become more self-monitoring.

Look–Say–Cover–Write–Check

Although at the beginning of the project many teachers knew of Look–Say–Cover–Write–Check, the systematic use of this approach was not really evident till later on. Look–Say–Cover–Write–Check did not work effectively where no clear guidance was offered to children as to when and how to work on spellings: many children were not clear what it entailed. As the project developed, this was a practice which was used to work on misspellings arising in children's writing, especially if the words identified were then linked to other words (e.g. words with similar patterns or structural features). Later in the project some of the older case study children mentioned that they used Look–Say–Cover–Write–Check in class and that it was one of the ways in which they had been helped to improve their spelling. They used the approach to work on words in their spelling logs. Look–Say–Cover–Write–Check worked best where teachers incorporated it into a classroom system or routine. A Year 5 teacher described how she established such a system in her class:

> I think after many years of teaching I've at last cracked this problem of collecting and working on individual spellings. It's only taken me 19 years! I help children to identify words they need to learn from their writing and they write them in their individual spelling book. We have a time each week to work on them using Look–Say–Cover–Write–Check. I also get each child to write the words on a piece of paper which I keep and update regularly. The children each have a spelling partner and they test each other every couple of weeks – they practise in between times – and then finally I check them. The more experienced spellers, who don't have so many misspellings, are encouraged to collect new words they want to spell and to work on those in the same way. It actually works! They've got their list and I've got mine, which is useful for me because you can't remember all that information. I've got a record of where a child is, any problems and how they are progressing. Now I feel I've cracked the time problem and the partnership issue. It's been something I've been working on for years. It's also made me look around and think about other ways of tackling spelling issues – some children with difficulties use a computer programme for collecting and spelling words.

Teacher intervention in children's writing and spelling

At the beginning of the project, evidence of teacher intervention in children's writing and spelling was very variable. There was real doubt, among some teachers, about the value of writing on or marking children's work, particularly that of younger children. Over the three years of the project however, this area began to be addressed more consistently particularly in Key Stage 2. This may have initially arisen through the spelling project inservice training sessions, but was also related to the increasing demands of Ofsted and LEA inspections.

There seemed an important distinction to be made between formal 'marking' for evaluative purposes, and informal teacher interventions which were more focused on moving children on. At its best, teachers' intervention and marking provided a helpful record of both children's work and teaching points. Teacher intervention at Key Stage 1 tended to be carried out alongside children during writing sessions, in particular where the teacher worked with a group of children. At Key Stage 2, intervention took place most effectively during writing sessions but often was carried out after the event.

These issues are thus best considered separately in relation to Early Years and Key Stage 1, and Key Stage 2.

Early Years/Key Stage 1

In the early years and at Key Stage 1 teacher intervention was mainly focused on supporting children at the early stages of independence in writing and spelling. Teachers supported children in the following ways, according to children's needs:

- by scribing part or whole of a text for children;
- by writing out the text under 'strings of letters' for children who had not begun to take on the spelling system;
- by writing standard spellings over selected words – particularly those close to the standard spelling;
- by identifying words spelled almost correctly;
- sometimes teachers would tick every correct letter in a word to offer encouragement and guidance;
- by drawing children's attention to capitalisation and punctuation.

In general teachers did not encourage children to copy writing – the main aim was to encourage them towards independence. Hence teachers preferred to write out what the child had written *after* the child had attempted to encode their message. In some classes, as outlined earlier, Early Years teachers organised their writing sessions so that they could work with one or two groups of children while other children either wrote independently or got on with other activities. This approach was incorporated into the guided writing section of the literacy hour. In the project, teachers usually worked with children at different levels of experience within the same group.

Year 2–Year 6

From Year 2 to Year 6 issues involved in teacher intervention and marking children's work became more complex. The following table (Table 6.1) examines many of the principal issues highlighted in teachers' interventions and marking, drawn from a review of all the writing samples from 6 case study children's writing (Years 2–6) over the three years of the project.

Initially it was apparent that teachers had very individual styles of intervening in or marking children's writing. At the minimalist end of the continuum one or two teachers would only tick work, without making a comment. Misspelled words were simply underlined or circled, and punctuation was corrected without comment. In addition, a substantial number of pieces of children's writing bore no evidence of teacher marking or intervention at all.

At the beginning of the project, general comments on a piece of writing would tend to be simply evaluative, such as 'good work', 'well done'. Later on, in years 2 and 3 of the project, comments which praised children grew much more frequent but were also more frequently accompanied by comments which showed teachers intervening in the following ways:

- responding as readers;
- helping children to structure or revise their writing;
- praising children for their use of language.

Analysis of teachers' interventions specifically connected with children's spelling showed a number of trends. In general, where there was a high number of misspellings, teachers seemed to stick to the principle of identifying a few words for correction and these tended to be commonly occurring words. Some teachers seemed unsure why they were identifying some misspelled words and not others, when marking a piece of writing. On occasion a relatively rare word would be identified as a misspelling while commonly occurring words like *thay* (*they*) or words where there was a common pattern of error (e.g. words ending in *-ed* written as ending in *-d*) were ignored. From this evidence it was possible to say that

Types of intervention/marking which decreased over the three years of the project	Types of intervention/marking which increased over the three years of the project
General interventions	*General interventions*
• No marking or interventions at all; ticks only • Simply evaluative comments (e.g. 'good')	• Teacher responding as a reader (e.g. 'I liked the part where...'; 'This is an exciting read...') • Comments on structure or plot of a piece of writing • Encouraging editing/redrafting • Comments on use of language • Comments on presentation • Evaluative comments alongside other kinds of comment (e.g. 'Good work, you've used paragraphs well in this piece')
Spelling	*Spelling*
• Teacher rewriting whole piece/section using standard spelling • Simply circling/underlining misspellings • Teacher correcting spelling by writing in individual letters on the top of the child's writing • Words for correction selected without any clear rationale • Asking children to write out spellings 3 times	• Drawing attention to particular spelling patterns (e.g. -ought in thought) • Identifying misspellings more systematically (e.g. words with particular patterns or features such as -ed, topic words) • Drawing attention to grammatical features of spelling • Encouraging children's involvement in their own spelling
Grammar and punctuation	*Grammar and punctuation*
• Correcting punctuation without comment • No comments on use of Standard English, grammatical aspects of spelling	• Comments linked to use of punctuation and paragraphing • Advice on Standard English • Helpful comments on grammar, word meanings and structures

Table 6.1   Changes in teachers' interventions in children's writing in Key Stage 2 over the three years of the project

some teachers were unsure about the purpose of intervening in children's spelling.

In years 2 and 3 of the project, as well as continuing to identify commonly occurring words, some teachers began to focus more precisely on different aspects of the spelling process. They began to draw children's attention to particular spelling patterns, grammatical features of spelling, specific topic words and in particular to actively encourage children to work on particular words. However, most teachers still mainly identified misspellings in commonly occurring words.

The perceptiveness of a teacher's comments on spelling was usually linked to the perceptiveness of their response to the writing as a whole. The most effective teachers looked for children's strengths and needs and considered how to move them on, rather than perceiving spellings as simply right or wrong.

Ways of learning to spell new words

Some teachers managed to incorporate a variety of strategies for spelling new words into their teaching and discussed these with their classes:

> Another thing we do is to look at a word for 13 seconds and learn it. I encourage children to break words down in their own way – we've talked about different ways of doing it. They enjoy doing that.
>
> With words like *does* – we've got some children that still write *dose* – we invent mnemonics like Dumb Old Elephants Sing to help them remember. Everyone enjoys coming up with those.
>
> (Year 5 teacher)

The approaches included encouraging children:

- to use a mixture of what they can hear, their knowledge of probable letter patterns, and word meanings;
- to make analogies from known words (e.g. if you can spell *night* you can spell *might*);
- to syllabify longer words;
- to draw on rules or generalisations where helpful (e.g. consonant doubling);
- focus on word roots or families, e.g. medic-ine and medic-al;
- to use 'over-articulation' to exaggerate the shape of the word (e.g. *Wed-nes-day*);
- to use mnemonics and other strategies to memorise problematic spellings (e.g. pap*er* is station*ery*; a *car* is station*ary*);
- to list the ways in which a word might be spelled, and then to make decisions about which version is correct.

Throughout the project, spelling tests were a source of discussion and were used by many teachers even though it was noted on many occasions that children did not always transfer their knowledge of how to spell words from tests to their independent writing. Some of the Key Stage 2 case study children, particularly those who were experienced readers but poor spellers, specifically mentioned that spelling tests which incorporated words with similar features had been useful to them.

Testing seemed to be effective when it was informal and linked to children's needs (i.e. when it was not based on arbitrary lists). Effective testing often involved:

- working with a spelling partner, or some form of self-review format such as Look–Say–Cover–Write–Check;
- a focus on a particular spelling pattern – this was found particularly helpful by children who were competent readers but who had difficulties with spelling;
- a focus on a particular group of words from a topic or core book;
- being used as part of a range of approaches not as the primary approach to learning new words.

Word study

During the project teachers increasingly highlighted aspects of spelling which drew attention to words – in particular their meanings and structures – through regular writing and word study sessions. In order to extend children's written vocabulary some teachers helped children to focus on word meanings through:

- creating word banks
- encouraging searches for alternative words through class activities and word study
- using thesauruses

Continuing attention to extending children's vocabulary of known words, including common words and words commonly misspelled in their writing, was an important aspect of developing their confidence.

As the project developed teachers increasingly displayed charts and lists of words which related to class activities in all areas – common letter patterns, word roots, webs of words sharing the same prefix, words which expressed shades of meaning.

> If we're starting a topic we look at words and we break them down for example yesterday we looked at 'photosynthesis'. Were there any parts of the word they recognised? We talked about words like 'photograph' and the link with light.
> The main thing is to get them interested in words and how they're spelling them, rather than seeing spelling as a chore.
>
> (A Year 5 teacher)

We had a word study session on prefixes. Then I asked the class to collect words beginning with the prefixes mis-, un- and inter- We made them into posters and hung them up for people to refer to.

(A Year 6 teacher)

Many teachers began to create posters for special vocabulary relating to new topics. For example one class had made a special collection of words relating to the class topic, rivers.

Spelling journals

One of the approaches recommended to teachers in the project was that children's work on spelling be incorporated into spelling journals where rules and hypotheses could be investigated, words with similar features collected, and meanings explored. This was felt to be preferable to generating many different worksheets, as it encouraged children in self-monitoring, and would provide a good record for teachers and children of their spelling progress.

Resources and their use

Providing a range of resources for spelling played an important role in promoting spelling development. From our initial observations in the project it was clear that there was a wide variation in the range, quality and use of resources for spelling. For example there was great variation, from Year 2 upwards in the quantity, range and availability of dictionaries and the ways in which children were helped to use them. Some classes had enough dictionaries for at least one between two children, as well as other dictionaries (from picture dictionaries to adult dictionaries and thesauruses) in the class library. In other classes it was sometimes hard to locate the few dictionaries in the classroom.

Use of the dictionary seemed to be most effective in Key Stage 2 when it was part of the editing and self-correction process. In one or two classes we observed writing sessions where use of the dictionary for editing was being specifically encouraged and developed. Some teachers taught children how to use a dictionary efficiently through the use of headwords and other features; other children were less sure of how to do this.

Many of the best resources were made by teachers and/or children and were linked to particular focuses for teaching:

- In a Reception class, there was a focus on the picture book *Mr Gumpy's Outing*. There was a wall frieze illustrated by the class which told the story. The teacher had written the words from *Mr Gumpy's Outing*: 'river', 'cow', 'chicken', 'children' etc. These were available to support children in their writing and for playing games. Each member of the class had written a Mr Gumpy zig-zag book and these were hung on a line across the classroom.
- In a Year 1 classroom a teacher wrote commonly occurring words on bubbles of yellow card which were attached to a display by masking tape. Children were encouraged to search on the display for words they needed – they could be removed from the display if necessary. The words also provided a focus for classroom activities based on known words.

In addition it is vital to demonstrate to children how resources should be used.

The writing area's always promoted as the most important area in the classroom. When there's children-initiated work going on, I'll always say 'Who's going to work in the writing area first?' and it's the most popular area in the classroom, definitely. I try and make it as attractive as possible with an inviting range of resources – different kinds of paper, books, borders, pencils, pens, everything clearly marked, name cards that they'd used over the year (and they've used them in all manner of ways – to make registers for instance), examples of handwriting, tracing paper, rulers, materials to make puppets to support their stories. Lately they're writing so much – self-initiated writing – and not just what 1 ask them to write, right across the curriculum.

(Year 1 teacher)

At Key Stage 2 there were many examples, later in the project, of charts arising from class word study investigations which reflected work in progress: such as words linked by particular patterns, words with the same prefix or suffix, words with the same meaning.

Key contexts for teaching spelling

Our observations during the project showed that there are several key classroom contexts for teaching spelling:

- the main routines of literacy teaching such as shared writing and reading and group reading;
- planned writing sessions where teachers support children's writing and spelling development at a class, group and individual level;
- during teachers' interventions in individual children's writing;
- through routines which establish independence in spelling, such as ways of learning new words, use of Look–Say–Cover–Write–Check, editing work, the use of dictionaries and thesauruses;
- word study activities which build on children's existing knowledge and may include both specific teaching, group and individual investigations. For example, at Key Stage 1: focusing on initial sounds and letters; studying particular letter patterns, rhymes and wordplay;
- while monitoring progress.

The role of parents

All the children with whom we worked in the project told us, in the course of conversation, how parents – often mothers, but also other family members – took an active interest in their spelling progress. Family involvement in children's spelling development occurred right across the primary age range:

> My mummy taught me at home so I was ready for school. She told me how to write properly.
>
> Lydia (Reception)

> If I'm at home I ask Mum and Mum says, have a go at sounding it out. My mum's a bookworm. She knows every word, so I ask her how to spell.
>
> Morgan (Year 1)

> On Saturdays when my mum doesn't go to work she teaches me a lot – spellings (and times tables).
>
> Shareen (Year 3)

> In Italian my dad always says to me – you write how things are said – and it isn't true because they use double letters everywhere and I get confused with Italian and English.
>
> Anna (Year 6)

> My cousin used to come round – I was about 6, he was about 13 – and read with me, and he used to bring a dictionary, let me look at the words first, then spell them out to him.
>
> Eliot (Year 5)

> At home I mostly use the dictionary to check on words but Mum often gives me the first three letters.
>
> Warren (Year 6)

As with children's reading it is clear that parents can play an important role in supporting development. For most parents whose own educational experience tells them that a word is either 'right' or 'wrong', looking at their children's early attempts at writing can be a relatively new experience. It seemed important therefore that schools have a policy for working with parents on spelling which:

- informs parents about the nature of children's spelling development;
- shows how a school is promoting achievement in spelling;
- offers ways for parents to support their children.

Part of the project involved collaborating with each school in the writing of a pamphlet for parents. A pamphlet was written jointly and schools then adapted it according to their individual context.

The literacy hour

The main teaching contexts of the literacy strategy – shared reading and writing, word and sentence level work, guided reading and writing, and opportunities for independent and group work – offer valuable opportunities for all the main teaching approaches discussed in this chapter, and to focus attention on spelling. In addition many schools are developing opportunities for extended writing, setting aside time for one or two writing workshops per week in addition to the literacy hour. Amidst the many 'word' level teaching objectives in the literacy strategy framework, it is important for teachers to develop and maintain key routines for teaching spelling such as opportunities for children to edit their work, reflect on their spelling strategies and tackle problems, and opportunities for teachers to focus on the needs of individuals and groups.

The effective teaching of spelling

We have summarised the findings of the research in relation to the teaching of spelling in two sets of guidelines which follow: one for KS1 and one for KS2. These guidelines provide a clear and easy-to-read guide to effective teaching approaches under four main headings:

- Key classroom contexts for teaching spelling (including resources)
- Major classroom routines for teaching spelling
- Class and group activities
- Routines to establish independence in spelling.

Taken together, the guidleines form the basis for a school approach to teaching spelling. A continuity of approach is essential in this area (as in others) if children are to consolidate their learning and make progress throughout their primary schooling. But the teaching of spelling also needs to be seen in the context of the teaching of literacy as a whole. As our research has shown, spelling is most effectively supported in a climate where children's experience as readers and writers is broad, where progress is carefully monitored, and where a real interest in words and language is fostered.

Teaching approaches for spelling: Reception and Key Stage 1 (ages 5–7)

Classroom contexts

The main routines of literacy teaching especially shared writing and reading, group writing and reading sessions, (generally as part of a literacy hour) are all valuable contexts within which children's attention can be directed to words and their spellings. Other key contexts at text level will include:

- promoting a wide range of extended writing
- teacher response to children's independent writing and spelling
- monitoring progress; assessment in writing and spelling.

At word level, there are many possible contexts for teaching spelling:

- explicit teaching which promotes problem-solving and analogy-making as part of word level work and word study
- investigative word study activities involving wordplay, rhyme, knowledge of letters and sounds, and word families
- activities across the curriculum e.g. looking at meanings and spellings of specific words in maths and science.

Spelling resources

A wide range of resources for spelling is a fundamental means of promoting spelling development. It is vital to demonstrate to children how these resources can be effectively used as part of their own writing routines:

- alphabet cards and strips to support writing;
- a range of alphabet books and early dictionaries;
- name cards showing names in upper and lower case;
- days of the week/month charts;
- small desktop word banks of other common words;
- word banks from core books and class topics on display;
- collections of words with common initial letters, rhymes, letter patterns;
- computer software which promotes attention to letters and words (see *Using computers*).

General classroom resources

Writing resources
These include:

- an easel, paper and large pens for shared writing;
- a range of papers, pens, pencils, stencils, small pre-prepared books;
- access to computers;
- charts with examples of handwriting style showing letter formation with 'exit' stroke guide rules.

A range of books

Because children will learn so much about spelling from their reading, the range of books provided in the classroom is important as a spelling resource. Books for shared reading and for paired, group and individual reading are the most important way in which children encounter a range of written language. Word banks based on some of these books will promote children's interest in words and their progress as 'noticing spellers'.

Display and classroom environment

The publication and display of children's writing, beginning with their earliest attempts, celebrates their achievements and also signals high expectations of writing and of presentation. Displays might include:

- writing from home;
- displays of shared writing and big books made by the class;
- children's writing in English and other community languages;
- children's own books 'published' in different ways;

Labelling in English and in other home languages

Making labels and signs provides an opportunity for discussion about the similarities and differences between languages and scripts, and gives status to the languages of all children in the class.

Writing corners and dramatic play corners

These can be resourced to encourage independent writing. Writing corners can contain basic writing resources handwriting charts and word banks. Dramatic play corners can provide children with materials for writing in role, and word banks related to their theme.

Major classroom routines for teaching spelling

Shared text work

Shared writing with an easel or whiteboard, where all can see the text, can take a variety of forms:

- making lists, writing signs, notes and letters;
- retelling stories based on favourite books;
- recording, or making up, songs and rhymes;
- writing across the curriculum.

For the purposes of teaching spelling, there may be an explicit focus for a session e.g. a rhyming pattern or a particular letter string

Shared and group reading

Shared reading using big books (both commercially published and classroom made) is a key opportunity for promoting an interest in words: their use, meanings, spellings and structures. Introducing a range of books ensures that children meet a wide range of vocabulary within different genres, which supports both writing and spelling development.

Opportunities for writing

Structured writing sessions, or writing workshops, should take place two or three times a week, both within and outside the framework of a literacy hour.

They provide opportunities for teachers both to demonstrate writing and to work intensively alongside groups of children on all aspects of the writing process.

Collaborative writing

Children can be encouraged to write in pairs to create a shared text (e.g. a letter, a set of instructions) either in structured writing sessions or as part of curriculum work. This gives them an opportunity to pool their spelling knowledge.

Informal writing in play

Play activities provide an important impetus to write, especially in the early stages. Dramatic play corners can contain resources which encourage children to write in role e.g. in a café, post-office, shop, hospital etc.

Handwriting teaching

Handwriting teaching, particularly in groups, helps children to establish the correct shape and formation of letters and to practise common letter patterns:

- Short frequent teaching and practice sessions are most effective.
- Each letter should be introduced with demonstrations of how it is formed (the teacher needs to demonstrate with her back to the children). Children can trace the letter in the air before practising it on paper.
- Letter recognition can be supported by multisensory approaches such as modelling plasticine letters, tracing in sand, making letters from playdough, using templates
- Letters can be taught in groups according to their formation, e.g. i l t u y/r n m h b p k/c. a d g q o e/s f/v w x z j or according to frequency of use by teaching common letters first, such as i, t, p, n, s.
- Always teach letters using the exit stroke – to allow for ease of joining (Sassoon, 1990; Jarman, 1990).
- Later on use letter strings and patterns which link to a weekly focus in handwriting practice sessions.
- Alphabet strips (lower and upper case) using correct letter formation should be on children's tables during writing later, well known songs, rhymes, poems and proverbs can be used for practice.

Using computers

Computers can be used to encourage children's early mark making, name writing, letter formation and, more broadly, their writing:

- Drawing software packages such as *KidPix Studio Deluxe* or *Dazzle 03* can provide enjoyable opportunities for mark making and 'drawing' letters in Reception classes using onscreen pencil, paintbrush, typewriter, and stamp pad.
- The act of writing on screen provides an added stimulus for many children for thinking about letters and words. Software which promotes children's confidence and enjoyment in writing such as 2Simple's multimedia *2Create a story* provides high motivation within easy to use software. Alphabet keyboard stickers from *Inclusive Technology* using lower case letters are sometimes helpful for children in the early stages.
- Sherston Software's abc-CD special edition provides opportunities for playing with the names, shapes and sounds of letters.
- Use of an interactive whiteboard (IWB), if available, can provide opportunities for focusing on spelling in the context of shared writing where the class can discuss how words are spelled or as a word level focus within a shared reading session look at particular word features – for example highlighting words which end with similar rhyming patterns. IWBs can also be used to create word banks which are the result of class discussions: these can be printed and displayed in the classroom or used on children's tables to support writing.
- 2Handwrite (from 2Simple software) allows children and teachers to create short 'videos' of handwriting movements.
- *Starspell* (Fisher-Marriott Software), is liked by teachers because of the links with the National Literacy Strategy and systematic progressive way of approaching all aspects of the spelling system.

Teaching approaches 5–7 years

Class and group activities to develop spelling knowledge in Key Stage 1

Phonological awareness

Whole class and group activities which focus on aspects of phonological awareness will support both reading and spelling development.

Syllabification: early stages

Hearing syllables in a word is the most fundamental aspect of phonological awareness:

- use names to clap out rhythms e.g. names such as Ja-son, Sha-mai-la, He-le-na, and favourite foods such as rice and peas;
- during shared writing or reading, focus on a particular word and tap out the syllables.

Awareness of rhyme

Awareness of rhyme can be encouraged by:

- singing songs and performing rhymes together as a daily classroom routine;
- choosing a rhyming pattern for the week and emphasising it in daily shared reading and writing sessions. For example:
  Eddy's off to find his teddy.
  Eddy's teddy's name is Freddy.
  (*Where's My Teddy,* Jez Alborough)
- using songs, rhymes and rhyming books (such as *Pass the Jam Jim*) which provide rich contexts for collecting onsets and rimes;
- using magnetic letters to build words and to show how different onsets can be added to rimes. Make a poster of words created;
- providing children with cards (with onsets in a different colour from rimes) and challenging them to make up as many recognisable words as they can.

Letter knowledge, knowledge of the alphabet

Names

For many children their name provides a basic initial repertoire of letters. Many children will be able to write their own name on starting school or nursery, others will need help to achieve this. They can be encouraged to use plasticine, playdough, sand, paint, cardboard and magnetic letters as well as writing to make their name. You can also:

- make a classroom alphabet book or frieze based on children's own names, using alliterative sentences. Books can have particular themes e.g. favourite colours, favourite animals (Annie's angry alligator);
- use children's names in as many ways as you can – make name cards for daily rotas and games;
- make collections of names, family names, names of characters on strips of card under the letters of the alphabet on a large wall display – these can be added to by children and discussed.

Alphabets

- Sing alphabet songs and rhymes.
- Involve children in creating their own alphabet books and friezes and encourage them to hunt for names, labels etc outside school. This approach is much more exciting than simply using a published book or frieze – although many of these provide excellent models e.g. *Eating the Alphabet.*
- Play alphabet games, e.g. 'I went shopping and I bought an apple, a ball', etc.

Developing a core of known words

Children need many opportunities to observe how familiar words 'work' (e.g. their own and others' names, words from a known core book) in order to see how to spell words for themselves. Much of written language in English is made up of relatively few commonly-occurring words. Children should learn to spell these correctly as soon as they are able. They can practise common spellings with the help of routines such as *Look–Say–Cover–Write–Check*. This can be introduced as a whole class or group game initially.

Other helpful activities include:

- reading and re-reading a core of familiar and well-loved books and making a word bank relating to a particular text
- book-based games, made from familiar books, provide opportunities for children to meet and observe particular words over and over again (e.g. a dice game based on *Owl Babies* which features the phrase 'I want my mummy' – see Helen Bromley *Book-based reading games*, CLPE 2000)
- once a week, ask children to write words they have learned to spell on a flip chart.
- create a big class dictionary/word bank of known words(*Our book of words we use a lot*) which can be added to week by week and be used as class resource.
- play 'pairs' and 'snap' games using familiar words or words from a core book

Moving on

Onsets and rimes

- Introduce common onsets and rimes, such as double consonant blends at the beginning of words, or common endings e.g. 'ing' to provide a focus for whole class and group teaching.

Onsets	Rimes
s	ing
st	ing
str	ing

- Common rimes, such as *-ack, -all, -ame, -ook, -ink, -ick, -ate* can be used to construct literally hundreds of words. Make a chart of common rimes with the children, and add to it (Wylie and Durell, 1970 cited in *Whole to Part Phonics*, page 9).
- Brainstorm and collect words with common onsets and rimes. Make big wall displays of words containing e.g. particular initial consonant clusters (such as *bl-, tr-, str-*). Children can be involved in hunting for and collecting these words.
- 'Snap' and 'pairs' games using different letter patterns can be played in groups.
- Use shared writing of songs, rhymes and poems to experiment with changing words and rhymes.

Common letter strings

Right from the start children can begin to notice names and other words where the spelling does not follow a 'straightfoward' phonic pattern. It is important to encourage children to look closely at words from the beginning, and not rely solely on phonic spelling strategies. Some groups of bilingual children whose first languages are written in more phonically regular ways may need particular help with the highly visual nature of the English spelling system.

- Use similar games and activities to those above, but this time focus on visual patterns e.g. -igh.
- Introduce the silent 'e' in creating long vowels and show how it operates regularly e.g. *at|e*, *man|e, pip|e, quit|e, rod|e, cub|e*.
- Build up words using magnetic letters during whole class sessions.
- Organise print hunts for words in which
    – the same letter patterns can represent different sounds: e.g. *oo* as in *food* and in *book*;
    – different letter patterns can represent the same sound e.g. *a* in *play, make, paid*.

Word structures

- Collect simple compound words – words made up of other words e.g. *football, birthday, afternoon*. This forms the beginning of work on word structures.
- Devise card games using words that can be combined to create other words for playing pairs, snap etc.
- In shared writing, discuss how plurals are formed, how the past tense is represented by an 'ed' ending, how we can change the meaning of a word by adding a prefix (un-) (the National Literacy Strategy support materials provide a range of examples).

Routines to establish independence in Key Stage 1

Encouraging children's independent spelling

- Children should be encouraged to use a variety of spelling strategies from the start: to draw on what they can hear and remember of words as well as using words known by heart.
- There should be a common approach to attempting unfamiliar words throughout a Key Stage.

At the very early stages, children who persist in writing 'strings of letters' will need individual encouragement to write down what they can hear and to represent sounds in words. At this stage, as well as supporting composition by scribing a child can be helped by:

- demonstrations, in shared writing sessions, of how to attempt unfamiliar words;
- teachers demonstrating word boundaries by writing under a child's string of letters;
- writing in collaboration with more experienced children;
- teachers providing standard spellings;
- shared writing in which children are active participants (e.g. groups where they take it in turn to offer spellings or to scribe).

Strategies for spelling

Help children to develop a range of spelling strategies, rather than simply advising them to 'sound it out':

- syllabification helps children to hear the syllables in words;
- analogy helps children to use words they know in order to spell new words: 'To spell a word we don't know, we think of a word we already know';
- children need to consider alternatives in encoding a word from sound into letter patterns e.g. is it 'nite' or 'night' and why?;
- mnemonics help children to find ways of remembering words e.g. what has a hat in it'.

Word books

- Using word books during writing (going to the teacher for 'words' which are then copied by the child) does not necessarily help children to develop positive strategies for remembering new words; it can lead to overdependence on the teacher.
- More productive is the practice of encouraging children to write what they can of a word and then use word banks and simple dictionaries to find and check these spellings.

Proofreading

- As soon as possible, help children to proofread their own work for spellings and to use personal dictionaries and word banks to help them. Demonstrate proofreading by using a piece of writing on a flip chart
- Encourage children to work in pairs on proofreading; this way they can pool what they know and discuss spellings
- As soon as they are able, help children to develop a checklist for proofreading such as:
  – Does my writing make sense and say what I want it to say?
  – Have I checked capital letters and other punctuation e.g. full stops?
  – Have I checked my spelling?

In this piece written by Samantha in her reception year, based on *Mr Gumpy's Outing*, her teacher has written standard spellings under some words. They are words which Samantha has spelled almost correctly.

Self-checking

List with the children sources of information about spelling which do not involve asking the teacher and put these on a poster eg:

- Think where you've seen the word before.
- Look in your personal dictionary.
- Ask a friend.
- Write out the word in different ways and think about it. Which one looks right? Now look it up.
- Look for the word around the room in an appropriate bank or list.
- Look in a dictionary – classroommade or published.
- These strategies can be demonstrated gradually in whole class sessions, and linked to particular teaching objectives (e.g. using the alphabet sequence in a dictionary or checking if a word looks right).

Responding and intervening

Teachers should respond orally to children's writing and spelling – written comments should reflect these spoken comments. Respond first to the content of a child's writing and, as children develop as writers, encourage them to read their writing aloud to partners, teacher, and the class.

Intervening in spelling

As soon as appropriate, identify words which are spelled almost correctly or words which contain common letter patterns, and help children to learn these thoroughly using Look–Say–Cover–Write–Check. Build on these known words and letter patterns in group and class teaching. Other interventions might include:

- scribing part or all of a text for young or inexperienced children;
- writing out the 'message' under children's 'strings of letters';
- writing standard spellings over selected words – particularly those which are almost standard and encourage children to learn them;
- drawing children's attention to capitalisation and punctuation.

Look Say Cover Write Check

Look	at the word carefully and mark any parts of the word which are causing you problems.
Say	the word to yourself.
Cover	the word and close your eyes. Remember the word by trying to see the word in your head. Say it slowly in a way that helps you remember how to spell it
Write	the word down, keeping it covered.
Check	the spelling to see if you have got it right. If you haven't try again or try working with your spelling partner

Teaching approaches for spelling: Key Stage 2 (ages 7–11)

Classroom contexts

Teaching spelling can take place in a number of classroom contexts, at whole class, group and individual level:

- as part of the main routines of literacy teaching;
- in many favourable working contexts e.g. children working with editing and spelling partners, teachers working or conferencing with small groups;
- when teachers intervene in and discuss children's writing;
- while teachers monitor progress and assessment.

At *word level*, children's interest in words and attention to their construction can be encouraged through:

- word study sessions – with planned focuses;
- focusing on word meanings, structures, origins and spellings in cross-curricular activities.

Spelling resources

Throughout Key Stage 2, there will be a greater emphasis on word meanings and structures in the teaching of spelling. Making and displaying the following resources will help children in becoming independent spellers. Teachers will also need to demonstrate how resources might be used, and to remind children to refer to them:

- word banks of common words;
- word banks from class topics;
- displays showing collections of words with common prefixes and suffixes (and their meanings);
- word banks of words using the same letter string (e.g. words using -*ough*);
- a range of dictionaries and thesauruses;
- a range of high interest alphabet books e.g. *I is for India*.

Computers

- Some spelling programmes (such as *Starspell*) can be a support for children at all levels of spelling development.
- Spell checkers are useful for children whose spelling is close to standard. Children with difficulties will need support in using these spell checkers.

General classroom resources

Resources for writing and bookmaking

Well-organised resources for writing and book making allow children to work independently, freeing the teacher to work with individuals and groups. You will need:

- a range of papers, pens, pencils;
- bookmaking resources;
- easel, paper and large pens for shared writing.

Word processing and ICT

Regular use of computers for word-processing enables all children to present their work to a high level. Children will benefit from access to:

- computers and word processing programmes which offer different fonts, colours and sizes;
- access to software which enables children to create multimedia texts.

Handwriting resources

A range of handwriting resources can help children to focus on presentation of their work:

- examples of handwriting style, showing letter joins;
- guide rules and borders;
- handwriting and calligraphy pens.

Display and classroom environment

Displays of writing

The publication and display of children's writing, in all the languages written in the classroom, celebrates achievements and also signals high expectations of writing and presentation.

Class libraries and book displays

At Key stage 2 the reading curriculum continues to provide vitally important models of written language which support children's writing and also their spelling development. Texts read should include a wide range of fiction, information books and poetry. Texts need to be displayed and organised in such a way that they are accessible to children, who understand the categorisation system in use. They can form the basis for word banks, drawn from favourite books, or related to curriculum topics.

Poetry books always have a particular role to play in drawing children's attention to language, and encouraging an interest in the sounds and structures of words.

Major classroom routines for teaching spelling

Opportunities for writing

Shared writing can be used by teachers at Key Stage 2 for teaching all aspects of writing and spelling in a wide range of written genres. At KS2 children will be able to participate very fully in the transcription aspects of shared writing, offering known spellings, working out how to spell unknown words, helping with scribing, and discussing punctuation and layout. Attention will increasingly be focused on the structures of words, their relationship to other known words, and their derivations and meanings.

Opportunities for individual writing

Children at Key Stage 2 need planned, regular opportunities to write in a range of genres, and to write at length. Through regular writing opportunities, children will continue to consolidate their knowledge of spellings, and to engage with a wide range of unfamiliar words and spellings. Basing some of children's writing on existing texts (e.g. through exploring a literary or information text in depth) helps to increase children's familiarity with written genres and to extend their vocabulary.

Writing workshops

A writing workshop approach can be fitted in to a literacy hour, and offers systematic opportunities for discussing all aspects of the writing process. Writing workshops provide opportunities for conferencing with groups of children. The structure of the workshop can be adapted to follow a literacy hour pattern:

- An opening whole class session where the writing is introduced by the teacher using a flip chart. This can include planning, listing, writing openings etc and can also be used to recap on work begun in a previous workshop. Spelling issues can be introduced at this point.
- Children move to writing individually working in pairs or in groups.
- A teacher can work with two or three groups during the writing time, focusing on compositional and transcriptional aspects of writing.
- A final plenary where the work of two or three children is read out, children respond to the writing, and particular points are chosen for discussion.

Collaborative writing and reading

Children benefit from working together on writing. This can take the form of creating shared texts, or of editing and proofreading each other's work. It is often helpful for children to work in pairs. Collaborative writing fulfils several functions:

- it enables children to pool their knowledge of writing and spelling and support each other;
- it allows them to observe each other's strategies;
- it helps them to articulate what they know and also to identify points that they are unsure of and need help with;
- it helps them to develop their sense of a reader, and to understand that their writing must be clear and comprehensible to an audience.

Shared and group reading

Many children do not automatically 'pick up' spelling from their own personal reading. Regular shared and group reading sessions provide a context in which teachers can draw attention to word meanings and spellings.

Teaching approaches 7–11 years

Word study

As children develop as spellers, the linguistic aspects of spelling – based on a knowledge of word structures and meanings – become increasingly important. Word study is interesting in itself and helps children to regard words as fascinating objects of enquiry, with their own histories. It also draws their attention to the syntactical aspects of language, and to the features of words which function as syntactical markers (e.g. the endings of abstract nouns; the way verb tenses are marked).

Handwriting

Cursive handwriting should be introduced by the beginning of Key Stage 2. This will necessitate regular handwriting practice sessions and practice can be linked to particular spelling patterns and word structures. Handwriting should also be linked to issues of presentation: final drafts of some pieces of work can be used for handwriting practice as can the copying out of favourite poems, songs or proverbs for class anthologies.

Using computers

Computers provide a variety of opportunities for developing children's competence as spellers in Key Stage 2.

- Wordprocessing in itself can be a valuable tool for reluctant writers or inexperienced spellers – for example the 'undo' button allows children to make more than one attempt at the same word. Automatic spellcheckers are effective in helping children to self-correct their own spellings. Children who teach themselves to type, including children who have spelling difficulties, can develop an understanding of the 'serial probability' of groups of letters. *Type to Learn Junior* is one example of software which supports children learning to type.
- Interactive White Boards (IWBs) provide an excellent tool for all kinds of interactive word level activities for whole classes and groups, as well as for looking at word features as they appear in texts – both read or written.
- There are many websites which provide support for spelling for use with a single computer or with whole classes using an IWB. Among these are:
  — Ambleside School, 'Look Say Cover Write Check' facility:
     www.amblesideprimary. com/ambleweb/literacy.htm;
  — BBC Spellits – which looks at a range of spelling strategies:
     www.bbc.co.uk/schools/spellits/;
  — Collaborative learning – which has a range of downloadable resources for teaching aspects of spelling, e.g. consonant doubling bingo:
     www.collaborativelearning.org/
- Online dictionaries, 'word a day' sites, rhyming dictionaries or thesaurus websites provide excellent resources for reference and word-study;
- Systematic support for spelling can be found from *Starspell* (Fisher-Marriott) and *Wordshark*;
- *Clicker5 (Crick Software)* and *Textease (Softease)* provide opportunities for writing with the support of multimedia word banks which support reluctant or inexperienced writers in Key Stage 2 and beyond.

Class and group activities to develop spelling knowledge in Key Stage 2

Spelling journals

Increasingly (and certainly from Year 3 onwards) spelling journals can be used for word and language study – to work on words with similar spelling patterns, to work out rules and generalisations, to define word meanings or record word webs. Journals can play an important role in promoting interest in spelling. For example, ask children to list as many synonyms as they can think of for a word like 'red'. They can add to their list from a thesaurus.

Spelling or word study journals can form a regular part of literacy hour routines and help to:

- reduce the use of work sheets;
- provide a place where children can record investigations into words and their meanings;
- give space to practise spelling points arising from children's own writing;
- provide an effective record for teacher and child of spelling development.

Letter strings and patterns

As children develop as spellers it is important to help them consider words with similar letter strings and patterns. These include words which look and sound alike and words which look alike but sound different. Collect words containing the same letter pattern, either as part of a planned focus or arising from children's work. Learning is more effective if children are actively involved in making the word collections, and in highlighting words with similar patterns and letter strings in newspaper articles (word hunts). Bilingual children will benefit from working with monolingual English speakers on these issues so that meanings and derivations can be discussed.

Examples of letter strings and patterns

- Words which look alike and sound alike:
  -ack as in sack, black, attack;
  -ust as in must, dusty, adjust;
  -igh as sigh, might, frighten, delightful.
- Words which look alike and may sound different:
  -ood as in good, food, wood;
  -augh as in laugh, taught, daughter;
  -ear as in tear, near, learn;
  -ould as in could, should, would, shoulder.

Computers can be used to make lists of words with similar patterns. Such activities can help children with spelling difficulties.

Focusing on word structures

Suffixes

Suffixes (the part of a word which changes meaning by being added at the end) form another important building block in understanding the English spelling system. Looking at how they are used helps children to understand the syntactical aspects of spelling.

Some common suffixes are:

-ism as in *terrorism, pluralism*;

-able as in *forgiveable, manageable*;

-ous as in *dangerous, fabulous*;

You can see whether children can generate other examples and explain what these suffixes tend to indicate.

Prefixes

Making collections of words with common prefixes can form the basis of investigative word study which can take place in whole class or group sessions, or with individuals using spelling journals. Some common prefixes are:

bi- as in *bicycle, binary*;

inter- as in *interview, intergalactic*;

mis- as in *misplace, mistake*;

tele- as in *television, telephone*;

Ask children to generate other examples of words that use these prefixes and think of other prefixes, together with examples and their meanings.

Creating word webs

Help children to analyse word structures by introducing simple word building grids. This helps children to develop rules and generalisations. For example what happens to the -y in the following words when the suffixes -ly and -ness are added?

sleepy, greedy, clumsy

Word webs can be built around words such as 'unhappiness'. In pairs children can be asked to generate (and note in their journals) as many words as they can which begin with *un-*, contain *happy* (*happi*)or contain the suffix *-ness*

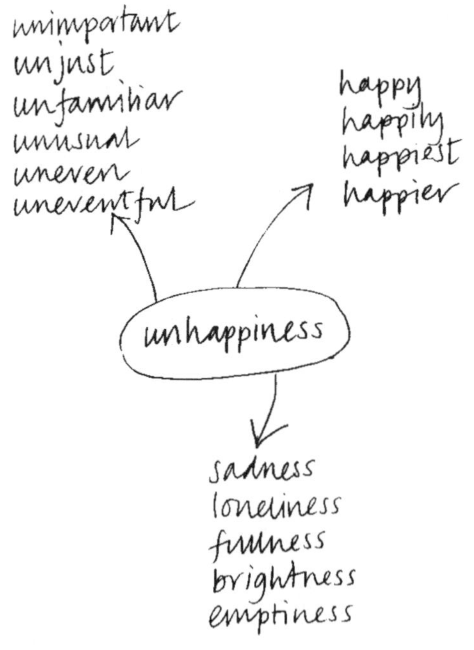

unimportant
unjust
unfamiliar
unusual
uneven
uneventful

happy
happily
happiest
happier

unhappiness

sadness
loneliness
fullness
brightness
emptiness

Figure 6.2

Helping children to look for rules and generalisations

Helping children to look for rules and generalisations is usually more effective than encouraging rote learning. Set up investigations and encourage children to carry out word hunts to test out their own hypotheses and some provided by you. The following might be useful areas to explore:

Rules and exceptions

- Is the rule 'i before e except after c' a helpful rule? Discover some words that follow the rule, and some exceptions.

Words using the suffixes -sion and -cian.

- Ask children to make collections under these headings, and to generate their own hypotheses about how new words are spelled. Do all words ending in -cian denote people in a particular trade? Test this hypothesis.

Words ending in ck and c.

- Help children to discover and formulate which words in English that end with a *k* sound, end in *-ck* and which end in *-c*. Do all words ending in -c have more than one syllable? Test this hypothesis.

Word meanings

At Key Stage 2 a collection of dictionaries (including etymological dictionaries giving word origins, rhyming dictionaries, name and place dictionaries, thesauruses, and dictionaries of phrases, proverbs and sayings) provide an invaluable resource for word and language study. You can set up investigations and activities based on these resources, for example:

- Discuss possible alternatives for particular words (synonyms) and encourage children to reflect on shades and nuances of meaning. A thesaurus will provide sets of words with related meanings which groups of children can be asked to discuss and differentiate between.
- Create word chains from compound words e.g. *snowfall/ fallout/ outside/ sideshow.*
- Word roots such as *sign* – as in resign, *signature, design, signal* – can be collected and word webs created around particular roots.
- Children can be asked to trace the origins of words such *woman, child, rotten, bag* (all Old English), *battle, pleasure* (Norman), *decimal* (Latin), *telephone, physics* (Greek), *bungalow* (Hindi), *anorak* (Inuit) – using an etymological dictionary. How have all these different words entered the English language?

(See Appendix 2 for suggestions for dictionaries, thesauruses and other resources.)

Routines to establish independence in Key Stage 2

Teach a range of spelling strategies

Teachers can help children to articulate a variety of strategies and to discuss ways of attempting, checking and learning spellings.

Encourage children to:

- write down what they can of unknown words using a mixture of what they can hear, their knowledge of probable letter patterns, and word meanings;
- syllabify longer words;
- make analogies with known words;
- draw on rules or generalisations where they are helpful e.g. consonant doubling;
- focus on word roots, families or meanings e.g. medic-ine and medic-al;
- use mnemonics to help with the memorisation of certain spellings;
- use 'over articulation' to help remember the word e.g. Wed-nes-day, Feb-ru-ar-y, gov-ern-ment;
- list the ways in which a word might be spelled, using what they know, and then make decisions about which version is correct, using the look of the word

Create a checklist of these strategies as a poster:

- to spell a word we don't know, we think of a word we already know;
- try out different ways of writing a word – which one looks right? Check it;
- if you have difficulty remembering how to spell a word, use an acronym to help you remember.

Teach the use of dictionaries

A careful approach should be planned for helping children to explore and use dictionaries:

- Alphabetical order can be explored by making themed alphabet books – an intriguing activity for older children as well as younger ones. A 'sports alphabet' (from archery to wrestling) or a 'London alphabet' (from Archway to Zoo) can be used to emphasise alphabetical order. The text can be brief or extended. Alphabet books can also be made as topic-related information books, using as models books like *A is for Africa*.
- Shared text work can focus on texts involving alphabetical order – telephone directories, address books, indexes, registers etc, and a class display can be made.
- Introduce the idea of dictionary quartiles

A B C D E F   G H I J K L
M N O P Q R   S T U V W X Y Z

and discuss why the last quartile has more letters in it than the others.
- Practise searching for a particular letter – using a three letter word such as dog. First find the quartile containing 'd' then find 'do', then 'dog'. Ask children to work with a partner and compare how many moves it takes to find a set of words.
- Introduce and practise the use of 'head words' in dictionaries.
- Compare definitions from different dictionaries and discuss which are better and why.

Standardise approaches to proofreading

- Proofreading their own and others' work is an important part of helping children to monitor their own spelling.
- At the earlier stages, or if it is difficult to establish editing partners, have an 'editing table' in the classroom where resources for checking spelling are kept and where children can check their spellings alone and with others.
- Encourage self-checking for meaning, accuracy of spelling and punctuation. Where possible children should be asked to circle words they are unsure of and to check these using personal and/or class dictionaries, word banks and lists.
- Encourage checking with a regular spelling partner before the end of a writing session.
- The teacher should check for errors – preferably in the context of regular conferences. Depending on the experience of the child, key spelling errors can be identified, strategies discussed and plans made for further development.
- Dictations can be used as outlined in the previous section to encourage children to use their strategies for having a go, self-correction, and self-checking.

Establish Look–Say–Cover–Write–Check

Develop a whole class system for using the Look–Say–Cover–Write–Check system for helping children to learn spellings:

- Identify a number of spellings in a piece of writing – this may involve both the teacher and the child. Words should be selected for a reason: because they are familiar words, because they contain a particular letter pattern or are topic words, because they are words the child frequently misspells or feels unsure about.
- Words can then be written into a Look–Say–Cover–Write–Check book or a spelling journal and are also written down by the teacher in a class book or a ring binder file with a page for each child
- Encourage children to syllabify words and to highlight the difficult parts of words.
- Children then practise the words on their own for one or two brief five to ten minute sessions per week, using Look–Say–Cover–Write–Check. They can also list other words using the same pattern, or re-visit words from previous weeks. This can take place during literacy hour time for independent work.
- Once every two weeks or so, children work with test partners to check their spellings.
- Every few weeks, the teacher can check the spellings as part of a group session.

Creating word banks

Word banks can be generated during whole class and group spelling sessions. Making word banks can involve children in brainstorming, using dictionaries, and attempting new spellings as the teacher scribes on a flip chart.

Word banks can be of different kinds:

- frequently used or frequently misspelled words arising in children's writing;
- topic word banks. For example one teacher had collected with her class words connected with their topic on rivers. A chart had been made with the word 'tributary', 'estuary', 'stream', 'delta' etc.;
- collections of words with the same prefix, and their meaning;
- collections of words with the same suffix;
- collections of words with the same letter pattern;
- collections of words, word webs and collections which are the result of investigations into a particular rule or generalisation.

Common words

Help children to remember commonly occurring words, if they are consistently misspelled. A chart of these common words can be available for reference, or children could make up simple card games based on such a collection, and play pairs or snap with them as an extra means of learning their spellings.

Informal spelling tests

Spelling tests can be helpful if carried out informally – in response to children's current needs or to classroom focuses such as:

- common letter patterns (including prefixes and suffixes). A familiarity with such patterns supports children in analogy making;
- words arising from children's own writing;
- words which children are continually encountering in well-known books and stories, topics, or areas of subject knowledge.

Short dictations can also be used occasionally to provide a way of monitoring progress. These are most effective if children have the opportunity to spend time reading and looking carefully at the text beforehand. Encourage them to focus on words they have previously had difficulty with, and get them to practise writing these words beforehand.

Chapter 7

Monitoring spelling

From the beginning of the CLPE/Mercers Spelling Project, an important consideration was to find a way of effectively tracking and analysing the case study children's progress over time. We aimed to develop a system for monitoring spelling development that would both serve the Project's monitoring needs and could also be easily used by teachers, and perhaps adopted for general use in schools.

Having considered systems for analysing spelling devised by Margaret Peters and Brigid Smith, and also by Mike Torbe, we arrived at a framework which was somewhat different in emphasis. Rather than focusing on older children or children with specific learning difficulties, as these other systems do, the CLPE Spelling Assessment Framework enabled us to look more objectively at the full range of spelling development, particularly of children in the primary age range. The framework not only gives a picture of children's developing spelling competences, but also provides a record of the range of strategies children are using, even in the early years.

The CLPE Spelling Assessment Framework can serve two main purposes:

- to record the spelling development of writers individually or across a class or year group, at the beginning and/or during a school year (for instance halfway through the year), in order to plan further teaching. (Use of the spelling framework is not particularly helpful until children have begun to use some phonetic strategies and/or some known words in their writing);
- to analyse the spelling of children who are experiencing difficulties, in order to monitor their progress and help devise appropriate teaching strategies. Frequency of use will depend on the child's progress and the time allocated for support.

The headings of the Spelling Assessment Framework

Standard spelling

The first column is the place to record all the standard spellings in the piece of writing being analysed. It is helpful to look at the percentage of standard spellings in children's writing over time. For instance, analyses of the younger case study children's samples of writing indicates that, once standard spellings form more than 90% of words written when writing independently, children can be said to have developed a sound understanding of the spelling system. Recording standard spellings is encouraging for both teachers and children alike, as there are invariably more words that are spelled in standard form than not.

This list of spellings that a child knows also provides teachers with an important resource: known words can be used to make explicit to children what they already knew about the spelling system. Additionally, they can be used to teach the making of analogies.

The remaining columns represent a spelling continuum, starting from the right-hand side and travelling to the left. The column headings provide a means of analysing the kinds of strategies which children are using in their spelling, by examining their misspellings or miscues. This analysis should be accompanied by discussion with the child, in order to discover which spelling strategies they believe they are using.

Pre-linguistic

Record here strings of letters, or spellings which show little understanding of the spelling system.

Early strategies: early phonetic and early visual

In these columns are recorded children's early attempts at spelling using the major sounds (such as beginning and ending sounds) in words (e.g. *pk* for *park*.) This is also the place to record attempts which show early visual strategies, where it is clear that a child has registered the general appearance of a word (e.g. *riev* for *river*).

Phonetic strategies

In this column are recorded spellings which rely predominantly on representing most of the sounds in a word (e.g. *disipolls*).

Developing strategies: structural and meaning strategies; visual patterns

- Structural or meaning strategies: these are misspellings which are linked to word meanings or to the ways in which words are structured (e.g. *intogalactic* for *intergalactic*).
- Visual patterns: these are spellings which draw on visual patterns of English spelling, even though the word in question is incorrectly spelled (e.g. *releaf* for *relief*).

USING THE CLPE SPELLING ASSESSMENT FRAMEWORK

1   List the standard spellings in the first column. Standard spellings can be recorded in two ways.
    (a) In the case of young and inexperienced writers:
        Record all of their standard spellings in the allotted section, even if a word has been used more than once.
    (b) For more competent spellers or for those who are writing at length:
        According to the amount written it is usually more practical to record only the standard spellings found in the first 60–80 words of the piece of writing and then to simply note the remaining number of standard spellings, before going on to analyse misspellings under the framework headings.
2   Then record each misspelling, exactly as the child has written it, in the appropriate column (you may need to write the standard spelling after some words). Don't be overconcerned about occasional difficulties in deciding where to place a particular word. A discussion with the child may help to clarify matters if the word is not clear.
3   Look at the columns. In which column do most of the misspellings appear?
4   At the bottom of the framework are spaces for totalling up numbers and percentages of words spelled in standard form, for totalling misspellings in each column, and for the overall totals (use of these numerical totals is optional).
5   The final section of the framework provides a space for the teacher to:
    (a) comment on what the analysis shows about the child's progress and identify any particular patterns in their spelling;
    (b) note any areas that require direct teaching.

Having analysed a particular piece of writing using the framework, it is usually possible to identify the child's predominant spelling strategies. According to the age and experience of the child, some strategies may be more appropriate and effective than others. For example, if the majority of misspellings fall in the phonetic column, then the teacher needs to consider how the child can be taught more about the visual aspects of English spelling and helped to observe patterns and structures in words. As Charles Cripps has frequently said, spelling development 'is about the quality of the spelling rather than the quantity of errors'.

Teachers' responses

Many teachers have helped to shape the CLPE Spelling Assessment Framework throughout its stages of development, by using it with children across the primary and early secondary phases. For children who were making good progress, even a very occasional use of the framework provided teachers with a picture of individual children's progress in spelling. With older children who were experiencing difficulty in spelling the framework was used more frequently in order to monitor progress and identify effective teaching and learning strategies.

Project teachers found this framework helpful in analysing what children were doing in their spelling. The following comments are typical of their responses:

> The diagnostic framework has helped me to really focus on the kinds of strategies children are using whereas before I just noticed the words weren't right
>
> (Year 1 teacher)

> The project has been very useful to me to help me think about strategies to improve my teaching of spelling. Filling in the framework is time-consuming but I would use it for some children. You get a real picture of a child's spelling.
>
> (Year 3 teacher)

> I think the diagnostic framework has particularly helped me. It's helped me to focus on specific stages of development and strategies, to see where a child is
>
> (Year 5 teacher)

The CLPE Spelling Assessment Framework can be found in Appendix 1 and may be photocopied for use in schools.

Points to consider in using the Framework

The following two examples of case study children's writing and analysis using the CLPE Spelling Assessment Framework show how the Framework can give insights into a child's progress in spelling, and indicate where teaching needs to be focused.

In using the Framework it is important to remember that the analysis relates to just one piece of writing and is therefore only one of the pieces of evidence which will contribute to the whole picture of the child as a speller. Other evidence may come from writing conferences and from observations during spelling activities. It is not necessary to address every point which arises from the analysis. You will need to consider the child's progress as a whole when listing areas for particular teaching.

Some teaching points arising from this kind of analysis can feed into whole class and group activities (e.g. ways of learning spellings; a focus on particular spelling patterns; teaching editing routines). In the example above from Lydia (Year 1) a teaching point which suggests collecting words ending with -*ly* could be shared with the class. She could also have been encouraged to practise they in her Look–Say–Cover–Write–Check book, and to make collections of words ending in -*ing* (she wrote *wige* for *wing*).

Lydia: a speller making rapid progress

Ladybirds

Ladybirds are good insects because thay it green flys. they have to. Wige case thay hibernate thay lay 1500 a day and they nest on rose boshes. and there have all kinds of lady birds. Ladybirds do not bite thay are very good insects I love lady birds thay are very nice insects thay there body have 3 prits to head neka body and thay are lovele hibernate to. thay inseects.

You have worked hard.

Ladybirds are good insects because they eat greenflies. They have wing cases they hibernate too. They lay 1500 a day and they nest on rose bushes. There have all kinds of ladybirds. Ladybirds do not bite they are very good insects. I love ladybirds they are very nice insects they have 3 parts to their body head neck body and they hibernate too. They are lovely insects.

This piece was written by Lydia at the end of Year 1. The analysis shows that she is making rapid progress as a writer and speller.

CLPE Spelling Assessment Framework

Name *Lydia*   Age   Year group *1*   Date/Term *June, Summer Term*

Languages *English*   Kind of writing *Information writing*

Words spelled in standard form	Structure and Meaning Visual patterns	Phonetic	Early		Pre-linguistic: little understanding of the spelling system
			Phonetic	Visual	
Ladybirds *on* (x5) *rose* *are* (x4) *there* *good* *have* *insects* *all* (x3) *of* *because* *do* (probably *not* given *bite* words) *very* (x2) *they* (x2) *good* *have* *I* *hibernate* *love* (x2) *nice* (given) *have* *lay* *to* *a* *body* (x2) *day* *head* *and* (x2)	*inseects (insects)* *greenflys* *case (cases)* *to (too) (x2)* *there (their)* *lovele (lovely)*	*thay x 8* *it (eat)* *boshes (bushes)* *cids (kinds)* *prits (parts)* *neka (neck)*	*wige (wing)*		

What does the analysis show about the child's progress in spelling (eg patterns of development)? Note any areas that require particular teaching

Lydia is making rapid progress as a writer and speller. She has been given a few words (the start of the first sentence) but also shows she has an extensive vocabulary of words she can spell – this is linked to her strong visual memory. She uses phonetic strategies occasionally (but 8 of these misspellings were the word thay.) She is generally consistent in her approach to spelling and is ready to consider a number of structural aspects, as well as to see patterns.

Total no of words 66

No of standard spellings 45

% of standard spellings 68%

No of miscues 21

% of miscues 32%

Thomas: a child with spelling difficulties

Some of the issues that arise from use of the Framework may relate purely to an individual (e.g. a child who has a particular difficulty). For example in a piece written by Thomas, in Year 3 (below), the analysis above showed that there were 32 misspellings in a piece of 65 words, an error rate of 49%. Using the Framework helped his teacher to identify particular points, amongst a wide range of errors, for Thomas to focus on.

It is clear from this example that Thomas needed individual support in developing effective spelling strategies. The bulk of his errors lie in the two phonetic columns and it is clear that his predominantly phonetic strategy for spelling is holding him back. The teacher notes the importance of helping him to make analogies where possible. At the same time he was helped by using *Look–Say–Cover–Write–Check* with a partner, to work on commonly occurring words.

Ones Ther wor a man Colld Roden he levd wev Iohn-Letl and a Foe uTher peple he Tile To ame at a Tree But the aroe Want UP in The air Note a pin-chon daw. and Note Roden on The hade Iohn-Letl had a go his Sot up in air Note an rotun apple SLat on his hade Then eve bode Luft

Once there was a man called Robin he lived with John-Little and a few other people he tried to aim at a tree but the arrow went up in the air knocked a pine cone down and knocked Robin on the head John Little had a go his shot in air knocked an rotten apple splat on his head Then everybody

Thomas was a moderately fluent reader who had difficulties with spelling. A summer born child, Thomas wrote this piece in Term 2 of Year 3 when he was 7 years 8

CLPE Spelling Assessment Framework

Name *Thomas*   Age *7 years 8 months*   Year group *3*   Date/Term *February, Spring Term*

Languages *English*   Kind of writing *Retelling a story*

Words spelled in standard form	Structure and Meaning Visual patterns	Phonetic	Early		Pre-linguistic: little understanding of the spelling system
			Phonetic	Visual	
a (x5) up (x2) *man in* *he (x2) (x2)* *and (x2) air (x2)* *to on (x2)* *at had* *tree go* *but his (x2)* *the (x3) apple* * then* * John* * (reversed* * J x2)* * an*	*Roden (Robin) (x2)* *ame (aim)* *aroe (arrow)* *hade (head) (x2)*	*ones (once)* *ther (there)* *wov (was)* *colld (called)* *levd (lived)* *wev (with)* *Letl (little) (x2)* *uthev (other)* *peple (people)* *want (went)* *pin (pine)* *ckon (cone)* *rotun (rotten)* *bode (body)* *luft (laughed)* *slat (splat)*	*tide (tried)* *note (knocked)* *(x3)* *sot (shot)* *eve (every)*	*daw (down)*	*foe (few)*

What does the analysis show about the child's progress in spelling (eg patterns of development)?
Note any areas that require particular teaching

Thomas is a good storyteller - and to his credit is prepared to take great risks with unfamiliar spellings. Still sees spelling as an arbitrary system although his reading is fairly well developed. Has a narrow range of known words which hasn't increased greatly. The bulk of his spelling errors lie in the two phonetic columns - however - not all his phonetic strategies are effective.

- *needs a great deal of individual support: conferences need to acknowledge what he already knows and to use this as basis for further teaching*
- *important to work with him on effective learning strategies ie making analogies with known words to create new ones eg went;*
- *work on strategies for learning commonly spelled words such as once, there, was - use Look-Say-Cover-Write-Check, working with spelling partner*
- *when he's ready, teach 'ed' as in verbs in past tense (colld, levd)*
- *start spelling journal with lists of known words to boost confidence and to use as basis for analogy making*

Total no of words 65

No of standard spellings 32

% of standard spellings 49%

No of miscues 33

% of miscues 51%

THE PRIMARY LANGUAGE RECORD WRITING SCALES

The CLPE Spelling Assessment Framework is essentially a formative assessment, but for the purpose of the CLPE Spelling Project we also needed a form of summative assessment whereby children's spelling development could be reviewed in the context of their writing as a whole. For this purpose we used the Primary Language Record (PLR) Writing Scales. These scales are helpful to teachers wanting to monitor children's spelling and writing development regularly. The full descriptions that they offer also contain indications of areas for further development.

- Writing Scale 1(ages 6–8) enables teachers to plot the progress of young or very inexperienced writers on a continuum from dependence to independence.
- Writing Scale 2 (ages 9–12) focuses on older/more experienced writers and summarises their progress as writers across the curriculum.
- Both scales describe the processes involved in becoming a competent and confident writer and speller.
- They can be used to monitor the development of individual children or of whole classes at particular points in the year.

DEPENDENCE

WRITING SCALE 1
(For children between the ages of six and eight)

1	**Beginning writer**	May be composing by dictating own texts, and may have some strategies for writing independently (e.g. drawing writing, copying, inventing own code), but still at an early stage of understanding how language is written down, and needing support with transcription.
2	**Early writer**	Gaining confidence in using writing for a range of personal purposes (e.g. messages, notices). Drawing on experiences of seeing language written down (e.g. in shared writing) and demonstrating more understanding of the alphabetic nature of the English writing system. Ready to have a go at writing independently, using a few early strategies for spelling (e.g. use of initial letters, some known words, using letter strings as 'place holders'), so that writing can be read.
3	**Developing writer**	Using a small range of writing (e.g. letters, lists, brief narratives) independently, but still needing help with extending and developing texts. May be drawing on models from reading in structuring own texts. Reading back own texts consistently, experimenting with punctuation, and developing strategies for spelling (e.g. known words, phonetically based invented spellings) which enable texts to be read by others.
4	**Moderately fluent writer**	Writing more confidently and developing ideas at greater length in a few familiar forms. Growing ability to structure these texts; willing to experiment with a wider range of writing. Beginning to use punctuation to support meaning (e.g. full stops, exclamation marks). Drawing on a wider range of strategies in spelling (e.g. common letters strings, awareness of visual patterns, as well as phonetically based spellings).
5	**Fluent writer**	Growing independence in using writing for a wider range of purposes (e.g. expressive, informational, imaginative). Aware of different audiences and beginning to shape texts for a reader. Often chooses to write over longer periods. Punctuating texts for meaning more consistently. Writing shows increasing attention to the visual patterns in spelling.
6	**Exceptionally fluent writer**	A confident and independent writer who enjoys writing in different genres, and is developing a personal voice. Writing may show marked influences of texts that have been read. Drawing on a range of effective strategies for spelling and using standard forms more consistently. Using written language in more deliberate ways and making meanings more explicit. Still needs support in sustaining long pieces of writing or expressing complex meanings.

INDEPENDENCE

DEPENDENCE

↑

WRITING SCALE 2

(For children between the ages of nine and twelve)

1	**Inexperienced writer**	Experience as a writer may be limited: may be composing orally with confidence but be reluctant to write or avoid taking risks with transcription. Needing a great deal of help with developing own texts (which are often brief) and with the writing demands of the classroom. Relying mainly on phonetic spelling strategies and memorised words, with few self-help strategies. Seldom using punctuation to mark meaning.
2	**Less experienced writer**	Increasingly willing to take risks with both composition and transcription. Writing confidently in certain genres (e.g. simple narratives) and trying out different forms of writing, drawing on experience of the models available. May find it difficult to sustain initial efforts over longer pieces of writing. Mainly using language and sentence structures that are close to speech. Spellings of familiar words are generally correct and attempts at unfamiliar spellings reveal a widening range of strategies. Using sentence punctuation more consistently.
3	**Moderately experienced writer**	Shaping writing in familiar genres confidently, drawing on experience of reading. Widening range of writing and taking on different forms more successfully. Aware of audience and beginning to consider appropriateness of language and style. Learning to revise own texts with support and to link and develop ideas coherently. Spellings of words with regular patterns are mainly correct and attempts at unfamiliar words show a growing knowledge of visual patterns and word structures. Using sentence punctuation appropriately.
4	**Experienced writer**	A self-motivated writer who can write at length and is beginning to use writing to refine own ideas. Developing own style and range as a writer but needing support with the structuring of more complex narrative and non-narrative forms. Likely to be reflecting on writing and revising texts for a reader, choosing language for effect or to clarify meanings. Using standard spelling more consistently and drawing on effective self-help strategies. Increasingly able to use punctuation, including paragraphing, to organise texts.
5	**Exceptionally experienced writer**	An enthusiastic writer who has a recognisable voice and uses writing as a tool for thinking. Making conscious decisions about appropriate forms and styles of writing, drawing on wide experience of reading. May show marked preferences for writing in particular genres. Able to craft texts with the reader in mind and reflect critically on own writing. Using mainly standard spelling. Managing extended texts using organisational structures such as paragraphing and headings.

↓

EXPERIENCE

Copyright © Centre for Language in Primary Education

Chapter 8

General conclusions and recommendations

Spelling, writing and reading

Despite all that is now known about the way children learn to spell and about available teaching strategies, spelling continues to be an area of controversy. We need to ask why this should be. One major issue that spelling always raises is the problem of error. Unless we limit children's writing only to what they already know, spelling inevitably entails embarking on the unknown. Children almost invariably make some errors when they attempt to spell words that they have not used in writing before. Their errors are there in black and white, evidence of imperfect learning, posing problems about how they can be effectively corrected. Errors in spelling are far more visible than errors in reading – to parents and public, as well as to teachers – and they are disturbing. Mina Shaughnessy (1977) remarked on the amount of energy and money that business firms and publishing houses routinely spend on eradicating error, whether by correcting fluids, scrapping drafts, or proofreading. Even in a highly computerised age this is true; in adult life our first response to an error is to erase it.

There needs to be a more general recognition that errors are a normal part of learning as children progress towards standard spelling. This seems to be a problem particular to the field of English. In Maths there is no similar expectation that children should always be one hundred per cent correct except in areas of rote learning such as times tables. Perhaps there is a misconception that spelling too is simply a rote learning exercise. Notions like this need to be corrected: spelling, like reading, involves the orchestration of many different strands of knowledge and is a skill which takes significantly longer to achieve than fluent reading.

Writing is the site where spelling is practised 'on the job', in many different learning contexts, for a variety of purposes. When children are encouraged to write they are given the opportunity to put their constantly widening vocabulary into active use and try out unfamiliar language. A frequent observation made by some of the older case study children in discussion was that, yes, their spelling was getting better 'but now I have to spell new harder words in my writing'. If we want children to develop as confident writers and spellers they need to be allowed to 'have a go' at unfamiliar spellings. But we should also be aware that active teaching can lead spelling development, enabling children to make increasingly informed first attempts at unfamiliar words.

Children learn to spell through writing but, as the case studies in our project showed, reading is also a site where a lot is learned about spelling – at word, sentence and text level. And the reverse is also true: spelling is a site where children make fundamental discoveries about sound-letter relationships. In fact there is now strong evidence that children's phonemic knowledge may develop initially through their spelling, rather than through their reading. This has implications for working with children at Key Stage 1. For instance, the National Literacy Strategy places a heavy emphasis on children's phonemic knowledge, but mainly in the area of reading. Teachers may find that sound-letter knowledge is more easily acquired and practised in the writing part of their literacy programme.

There needs to be more documentation of effective practice in this aspect of literacy where we often found teachers to be less than confident. Teachers need to be able to draw on a tried and tested range of pedagogical approaches in dealing with the diverse needs of children learning to spell.

Main findings

This book began by posing a number of questions about how children learn to spell. On the basis of our case study evidence we found that:

- children did not necessarily follow a linear model of development but drew on different kinds of knowledge from the earliest stages;
- children showed individual preferences in their spelling strategies – phonetic or visual – from the earliest stages;
- children all needed to broaden their range of the earliest stages strategies to make progress as effective spellers;
- when children began to make analogies with words they already knew in order to attempt unfamiliar spellings, they showed that they were beginning to be aware of spelling as a system;
- analogy-making involved them in paying attention to grammatical and linguistic features as well as sound-letter relationships;
- children's involvement and interest in the written word through reading and writing in the broadest sense provided the foundation for their becoming more proficient spellers.

The six case studies in Chapter 5 – three of children who were developing competently as spellers and three of children who were experiencing difficulties – showed how these findings related to individual children's histories.

Good readers, poor spellers

One of the areas we set out to investigate was the spelling development of children who were good readers and poor spellers. That this combination is a not uncommon one seems counter-intuitive: most people assume that reading is one of the main ways that children learn to spell. Why was it that these children – fluent and sometimes avid readers – were not making more connections between their reading and writing? Two of our case studies in Chapter 5 showed that, although confident readers, these children:

- did not make links between the words they could read and their spellings;
- may have attended only to partial cues in their reading and therefore resorted in their spelling to the most basic phonetic spelling strategies;
- thought of spelling as arbitrary in that they tended to see words as individual units and did not make links between familiar and unfamiliar words in their spelling.

These children were helped by:

- being encouraged to take an active and responsible role in their own development as spellers (e.g. through editing and self-correcting their writing, including working with a spelling partner);
- being helped to make connections at many different levels in order to develop their spelling knowledge (e.g. make analogies between words with similar rimes, visual patterns, word structures);
- having regular conferences with teachers who had analysed their spelling development and who discussed specific strategies with them;
- following helpful routines such as Look–Say–Cover–Write–Check;
- being helped to see themselves as writers and to develop their writing in spite of their difficulties with spelling.

Although there were only a few children in this project who could be categorised as good readers and poor spellers, there was a real concern within the schools about this discrepancy, which often created uncertainty in teachers. It seems important that this group of children should be identified and offered clearly focused support within classrooms, based on careful analyses of their difficulties. Blanket 'phonics programmes' would have been unhelpful to these children, who were already overdependent on phonetic approaches in their spelling and needed to address the visual, syntactic and semantic aspects of spelling in order to progress.

It is also important that teachers should distinguish between those children who are good readers and poor spellers and those who are experiencing difficulties in both reading and spelling. Children in the latter group have much less knowledge about the spelling system and their becoming more proficient spellers. need different kinds of support. Support for both groups should always be based on analysis of children's writing, spelling and reading.

The active teaching of spelling

Observations of and discussions with teachers showed that the active teaching of spelling played a decisive role in children's development. There were a number of approaches common to those classrooms where children were helped to make significant progress as spellers and writers. Effective teaching of spelling involved:

- generating a real enthusiasm for language – read, spoken and written – at text, sentence and word level;
- using the classroom literacy programme to discuss and demonstrate aspects of spelling in activities such as shared writing and reading;
- teaching spelling through a combination of working within the writing process (from shared writing to editing individual children's writing) and more explicit forms of teaching, where particular aspects of spelling were actively discussed and investigated;
- helping children from the early stages to develop a variety of spelling strategies – phonic and visual, to develop a sense of pattern through analogy making and to steadily acquire a vocabulary of known words;
- helping children to discuss and investigate the syntactic and semantic features of words; at the beginning of the project these were the aspects of spelling that were least acknowledged by teachers;
- responding to and intervening in children's writing in ways that helped them to move on as both writers and spellers;
- analysing children's spelling in order to gain insights into the spelling process and identify particular strengths and weaknesses;
- helping children to take more responsibility for and plan their own learning;
- sharing information with parents and involving them in school policy.

As the project proceeded and we worked alongside teachers and children, we intervened in two ways. We produced teaching guidelines, based on observations and discussions with teachers, and we developed a Spelling Assessment Framework (Chapter 7) which both helped the work of the project and enabled teachers to analyse children's progress as spellers. For some teachers, this Framework significantly helped their understanding of how best to support children's progress.

Suggestions for further work in this field

The special feature of our study was that it was longitudinal, following children's progress as spellers over three years of their lives in school. In this it was unusual: most studies of spelling, with a few honourable exceptions (e.g. Hughes and Searle 1997) do not look at children's spelling over time, but attempt to draw conclusions about development in this area from a selection of samples drawn from different age groups. It is clear that more work is still needed in this area – especially work which views spelling not as a discrete process but as part of children's learning of literacy. Our project was limited in its scope and we were unable to visit children's homes; future research needs to look in more detail at the links between home to school learning. In addition, children's acquisition of phonemic knowledge through their spelling and the relationship of this with their reading development, will be an important and topical question to consider: Uta Frith's model of reading and writing development which we drew on in Chapter 2 offers a powerfully suggestive framework for a longitudinal study.

It was clear from our case studies of children who are good readers and poor spellers that there is a need for further study of this group of children, but from an earlier stage in their development. When we met them in Key Stage 2 the children in this group had achieved reasonable fluency as readers, a fluency which had, for a while, diverted teachers' attention from their growing problems in spelling. By the time the divergence between their reading and spelling had clearly emerged they had missed out on some important learning opportunities.

This study has established that children's writing experiences, in the broadest sense, are integral to their spelling progress. While children were clearly helped by the active teaching of spelling, it was in their writing that children really engaged with the spelling system and this was where their real and actual progress could be observed. Where their opportunities for writing were limited, their spelling was also observed to regress. This was significant for teachers working within the literacy hour. Some interpretations of the literacy hour led to a decline in opportunities for writing in some classrooms, especially at KS2. Any restriction of children's opportunities for writing is likely to have a significant effect not only on their writing, but also on their learning of spelling.

We hope that this book will be a helpful tool for teachers and for pre-service and in-service education. All those with an interest in children's spelling development become better able to help them if they acquire a better understanding of what is going on as children learn to spell. For many people, spelling has not been an interesting aspect of literacy development. It has been spoken of as part of the 'mechanics' of writing and viewed as merely a 'surface feature', something that children get either wrong or right. We have tried to show that this is not so; spelling is a much more complex skill than at first appears.

Appendix 1

CLPE Spelling Assessment Framework

Name _____ Age _____ Year group _____ Date/Term _____

Languages _____ Kind of writing _____

Words spelled in standard form	Structure and Meaning Visual patterns	Phonetic	Early		Pre-linguistic: little understanding of the spelling system
			Phonetic	Visual	

What does the analysis show about the child's progress in spelling (eg patterns of development)?
Note any areas that require particular teaching

Total no of words _____

No of standard spellings _____

% of standard spellings _____

No of miscues _____

% of miscues _____

Appendix 2

Alphabet books, dictionaries and other useful books about words

Alphabet Books

Base, Graeme: *Animalia*, Viking 1986/Puffin 1990

Beck, Ian: *ABC Bookchart,* Walker 1991

Beck, Ian: *The Orchard ABC,* Orchard 1994

Bloom, Valerie: *Ackee, Breadfruit, Callaloo. An Edible Alphabet,* illus. Kim Harley, Macmillan Education/ Bogle l'Ouverture 1999

Brown, Ruth: *A Four-tongued Alphabet,* Andersen Press 1991/Red Fox 1992

Browne, Philippa-Alys: *African Animals ABC,* Barefoot Books 1995

Bunting, Jane: *My First ABC,* Dorling Kindersley 1993

Campos, Maria de Fatima: *B is for Brazil,* Frances Lincoln 1999

Carter, David A.: *Alpha Bugs,* Orchard 1994

Cave, Kathryn: *W is for World,* Frances Lincoln 1998

Chin-Lee, Cynthia: *A is for Asia,* illus. Yumi Heo, Orchard, New York 1997

Cohen, Izhar: *ABCDiscovery!,* David Bennett 1998

Cousins, Lucy: *Maisy's ABC,* Walker 1994

Crowther, Robert: *Most Amazing Hide and Seek Alphabet Book,* Walker 1999

Crowther, Robert: *My Oxford Pop-up Surprise abc,* Oxford University Press 1996

Das, Prodeepta: *I is for India,* Frances Lincoln 1996/ 1999

Dodd, Lynley: *The Minister's Cat ABC,* Spindlewood 1992/Puffin 1994

Ehlert, Lois: *Eating the Alphabet. Fruit and Vegetables from A to Z,* Harcourt Brace, USA 1989. Available in big book format

Grover, Max: *Accidental Zucchini. An Unexpected Alphabet,* Harcourt Brace, USA 1993. Available in big book format

Hughes, Shirley: *Alfie's Alphabet,* Bodley Head 1997

Hughes, Shirley: *Lucy and Tom's ABC,* Puffin 1986

Kitamura, Satoshi: *From Acorn to Zoo and Everything in Between in Alphabetical Order,* Red Fox 1992

Lester, Alison: *Alice and Aldo,* Allen & Unwin 1996

McDonnell, Flora: *ABC,* Walker 1997/1998

McGough, Roger: *My Oxford ABC Picture Rhyme Book,* illus. Debi Gliori, Oxford University Press 1994

MacKinnon, Debbie: *My First ABC,* photographs by Anthea Sieveking, Frances Lincoln 1992/1995

Micklethwait, Lucy: *I Spy: An Alphabet in Art,* HarperCollins 1992

Offen, Hilda: *The Bad Day ABC,* Hamish Hamilton 1996/Puffin 1997

Onyefulu, Ifeoma: *A is for Africa,* Frances Lincoln 1993/1995. Available in big book format

Patten, Brian: *The Blue Green Ark. An Alphabet for Planet Earth,* Scholastic Press 1999

Pollinger, Gina: *Alphabet Gallery. An ABC of Contemporary Illustrators,* Mammoth 1999

Dr Seuss: *Dr Seuss's ABC,* Collins 1964. Available on CD ROM: Broderbund Living Books

Simmonds, Posy: *F-Freezing ABC,* Cape 1995/Red Fox 1998

So, Sungwan: *C is for China,* Frances Lincoln 1997

Stickland, Paul: *ABC Bouncy Boxes and Board Book,* Ragged Bears 1995

Testa, Fulvio: *A Long Trip to Z,* Andersen Press 1997

Voake, Charlotte: *Alphabet Adventure,* Cape 1999

Wildsmith, Brian: *ABC,* Oxford University Press 1995 (originally published in 1962)

Wilson-Max, Ken:*L is for Loving. An ABC for the way you feel,* David Bennett Books 1999

Wood, Jakki: *Animal Parade. A Wildlife Alphabet,* Frances Lincoln 1993/1996

Dictionaries and Thesauruses

Oxford University Press (tel: 01865 267795) publish a wide range of dictionaries for different ages, including:

My Very First Oxford Dictionary (Available in a big book edition)

My First Oxford Dictionary

The Oxford Primary School Dictionary

The Oxford Primary School Thesaurus

Other useful dictionaries include:

Collins Emergent Dictionary

Collins Early Dictionary Collins Junior Dictionary

Collins New School Dictionary

Dorling Kindersley First Dictionary
Dorling Kindersley Children's Dictionary CD-ROM (Win)
Dorling Kindersley Children's Illustrated Dictionary
My First Incredible Amazing Dictionary CD-ROM (Win/Mac)
Dorling Kindersley
The Ginn School Dictionary
The Kingfisher Children's Illustrated Dictionary The Kingfisher Children's Illustrated Thesaurus
The Usborne Illustrated Dictionary
The Usborne Illustrated Thesaurus

In junior classrooms it is also a good idea to have an adult dictionary to allow for the limitations of children's dictionaries.

Books and resources for children

Beal, George: *Kingfisher Children's Book of Words*, Kingfisher 1999

Bryant-Mole, Karen: *English Keywords. Words and Sentences*, Wayland 1999

Clegg, Gillian; *Clues from Names*, Wayland 1998

Deary Terry: *Wicked Words (Horrible Histories)*,, illus. Philip Reeve Scholastic 1996

Hayes, Sarah: *Sound City*, illus. Margaret Chamberlain Walker 1998/1999

Palmer, Sue: *A Simple Rhyming Dictionary*, (Pelican Big Book) Longman 1998

Palmer, Sue: *Words Borrowed from Other Languages*, (Pelican Big Book) Longman 1998

Young, Sue: *The Scholastic Rhyming Dictionary*, Scholastic, USA 1994. This dictionary needs to be used with care with regard to spelling due to its American origin, but is included here because of the dearth of rhyming dictionaries available in the UK, especially those accessible to children.

WordRoot, CD-ROM. Wordroutes Ltd. Tel: 01767 600580
My Oxford Word Box, CD-ROM Oxford University Press

Books written for adults (older children may find some of these useful)

Ellefson, Connie Lockhart: *The Melting Pot Book of Baby Names*, 3rd edition, Betterway Books, Cincinnati, Ohio 1995. Explains naming traditions from cultures around the world as well as giving the meanings of names.

Fergusson, Rosalind: *The Penguin Rhyming Dictionary*, Penguin 1985

Flavell, Linda & Roger: *Dictionary of Idioms and their Origins*, Kyle Cathie 1994

Flavell, Linda & Roger: *Dictionary of Proverbs and their Origins*, Kyle Cathie 1994

Flavell, Linda & Roger: *Dictionary of Word Origins*, Kyle Cathie 1996

Hoad, T F (ed): *The Concise Oxford Dictionary of English Etymology*, Oxford University Press 1993

McWilliam, Norah: *What's in a Word? Vocabulary Development in Multilingual Classrooms*, Trentham Books 1998

Rees, Nigel: *The Cassell Dictionary of Word and Phrase Origins*, Cassell 1996/1998

Room, Adrian: *Brewer's Dictionary of Names. People, Places and Things*, Helicon 1999

Room, Adrian: *The Cassell Dictionary of First Names*, Cassell 1995/1997

Room, Adrian: *The Cassell Dictionary of Word Histories*, Cassell 1999

Bibliography

Barrs, Myra, Ellis, Sue, Hester, Hilary and Thomas, Anne: *The Primary Language Record: handbook for teachers*, CLPE/ILEA 1988

Barrs, Myra, Ellis, Sue, Hester, Hilary and Thomas, Anne: *Patterns of Learning*, CLPE 1990

Bissex, Glenda L: *Gnys at Wrk: a child learns to read and write*, Harvard University Press 1980

Bryant, Peter and Bradley, Lynette: *Children's Reading Problems*, Blackwell 1985

Bradley, Lynette and Huxford, Laura: 'Organising sound and letter patterns for spelling' in Brown G and Ellis N (eds), *The Handbook of Spelling, Theory, Process and Intervention*, John Wiley and Sons 1994

Bromley, Helen: *Book-based Reading Games*, (forthcoming) CLPE

CLPE *Primary Language Record Reading Scales* in *Using the Primary Language Record Reading Scales, Establishing Shared Standards*, CLPE 1996

CLPE *Primary Language Record Writing Scales 1 and 2*, CLPE 1997

Cripps, Charles and Cox, R: *Joining the ABC, How and Why Handwriting and Spelling Should be Taught Together*, LDA 1990

DES: *English in the National Curriculum*, HMSO 1990

DFE: *English in the National Curriculum*, HMSO 1995

Dombey, Henrietta, Moustafa, Margaret and the staff of CLPE: *Whole to Part Phonics*, CLPE 1998

Ehri, Linnaea: 'The development of orthographic images', in Frith, Uta (ed): *Cognitive Processes in Spelling*, Academic Press Inc 1979

Ellis, N.: 'Longitudinal Studies of Spelling Development', in Brown, G. and Ellis, N. (eds), *The Handbook of Spelling, Theory, Process and Intervention*, John Wiley and Sons 1994

Fernald, Grace: *Remedial Techniques in Basic School Subjects*, New York: McGraw-Hill 1943

Ferreiro, Emilia and Teberosky Anne: *Literacy Before Schooling*, Heinemann, USA 1979

Frith, Uta: 'Unexpected spelling problems', in Frith, Uta (ed): *Cognitive Processes in Spelling*, Academic Press Incorporated 1980

Frith, Uta: 'Beneath the surface of developmental dyslexia', in Patterson, K. E., Marshall, J. C. and Coltheart, M.: *Surface Dyslexia: neuropsychological and cognitive studies of phonological reading*, Lawrence Erlbaum 1985

Gentry, J. R.: 'Developmental aspects of learning to spell', in Booth, David (ed.): *Spelling Links*, Pembroke 1991

Gentry J. R.: *SPEL...is a four letter word*, Scholastic 1987

Goodman Kenneth: *Language and Literacy: the selected writings of Kenneth S. Goodman*, edited by Frederick V Gollasch, 2 vols, Routledge and Kegan Paul 1982

Goswami, Usha and Bryant, Peter: *Phonological Skills and Learning to Read*, Lawrence Erlbaum 1990

Goswami, Usha, 'Phonological development and reading by analogy: what is analogy and what is not?', *Journal of Research in Reading*, Vol 18 (2), 1995

Goswami, Usha: 'Causal connections in beginning reading: the importance of rhyme', *Journal of Research in Reading*, Vol 22 (3), 1999

Harste, Jerome C., Woodward, Virginia A. and Burke, Carolyn L.: *Language Stories and Literacy Lessons*, Heinemann Educational 1984

Henderson, Edmund: *Teaching Spelling*, Houghton Mifflin 1990

Henderson, E. and Templeton, S.: 'A developmental perspective of formal spelling instruction through alphabet, pattern and meaning', in Booth, David (ed.): *Spelling Links*, Pembroke 1991

Hughes, Margaret and Searle, Dennis: *The Violent E and Other Tricky Sounds: Learning to Spell from Kindergarten through Grade 6*, Stenhouse 1997

Jarman, Christopher: *The Development of Handwriting Skills*, Simon and Schuster 1990

Lennox, Carolyn and Siegal, Linda S.: 'The role of phonological and orthographic processes in learning to spell', in *The Handbook of Spelling: Theory, Process and Intervention*, John Wiley and Sons 1994

Moustafa, Margaret: *Beyond Traditional Phonics. Research Discoveries and Reading Instruction*, Heinemann USA 1997

Mudd, Norma: *Effective Spelling: a practical guide for teachers*, Hodder & Stoughton/UKRA 1994

Payton, Shirley: *Developing Awareness of Print: young child's first steps towards literacy*, Education Review, University of Birmingham 1984

Peters, Margaret: *Spelling Caught or Taught*, Routledge 1985

Peters, Margaret and Smith, Brigid: *Spelling in Context*, NFER-Nelson 1993

Ramsden, Melvyn: *Rescuing Spelling*, Southgate 1993

Read C: *Children's Creative Spelling*,, Routledge and Kegan Paul, 1986

Sassoon, Rosemary: *Handwriting: the way to teach it*, Stanley Thornes Ltd 1990

Schonell, Fred: *Essentials in Teaching and Testing Spelling*, Macmillan 1932

Shaughnessy, Mina: *Errors and Expectations. A guide for the teacher of basic writing*, New York: Oxford University Press 1977

Slobin, D.: *Psycholinguistics*,, Scott, Foresman and Company 1971

Smith, Frank: *Writing and the Writer*, Heinemann, USA 1982

Snowling, Margaret: 'Towards a model of spelling acquisition: the development of some competent skills', in Gordon, D., Brown, A. and Ellis, N. C. (eds): *The Handbook of Spelling, Theory, Process and Intervention*,, John Wiley and Sons 1994

Stubbs, Michael: *Language and Literacy: the sociolinguistics of reading and writing*, Routledge 1980

Temple, Charles A., Nathan, Ruth G. and Burris, Nancy A.: *The Beginnings of Writing*, 2nd edn, Allyn and Bacon 1988

Torbe, Mike: *Teaching and Learning Spelling*, 3rd edn, Ward Lock 1995

Treiman, R: 'Sources of information used by beginning spellers', in Gordon, D., Brown, A. and Ellis, N. C. (eds): *Handbook of Spelling Theory, Process and Intervention*, John Wiley and Son 1994

Treiman, R., Mullenix J., Bijeljac-Babic, R. and Richmond-Welty, E. D.: 'The special role of rimes in the description, use and acquisition of English orthography' *Journal of Experimental Psychology, General*, 124, 107–36. 1995

Vygotsky, Lev: *Mind in Society: the development of higher psychological processes*, Harvard University Press 1978

Wylie, R. E. and Durell, D. D.: *Elementary English*, 1970, 47, 787–91

Children's Books

Alborough, Jez; *Where's My Teddy?*, Walker 1992/1994

Brown, Ruth: *A Dark, Dark Tale*, Andersen Press 1981/Red Fox 1992

Burningham, John: *Mr Gumpy's Outing*, Cape 1973/Puffin 1978

Burningham, John: *The Shopping Basket*, Cape 1980/Red Fox 1992

Das, Prodeepta: *I is for India*, Frances Lincoln 1996/1999

Ehlert, Lois: *Eating the Alphabet*, Harcourt Brace, USA 1989

Ermest, Kate Elizabeth: *Hope Leaves Jamaica*, Methuen 1993/Mammoth 1994

Onyefulu, Ifeoma: *A is for Africa*, Frances Lincoln 1993/1995

Umansky, Kaye: *Pass the Jam, Jim*, illus. Margaret Chamberlain, Bodley Head 1992/Red Fox 1993

Ure, Jean: *William in Love*, Puffin 1993

Waddell, Martin: *Owl Babies*, illus. Patrick Benson, Walker 1992/1994

Computer software

Starspell (1999) Fisher-Marriott Software, 58 Victoria Road, Woodbridge IP12 1EL

Index